SUSHI COOKBOOK

101 DELICIOUS SUSHI RECIPES FOR BEGINNERS TO MAKE SUSHI AT HOME

Table of Contents

CHAPTER 1: BREAKFAST RECIPES

SUPER-FOOD SUSHI ROLLS (2 SERVINGS, SERVING: 1 PORTION)

Per Serving, Calories: 338- Fat: 12.5g - Carbs: 57.3g - Protein: 6.7g

Ingredients:

- 2 hard stems removed kale leaves

- 3 tbsp. of cashew butter

- 2 peeled bananas

- 2 tsp. of agave nectar

- 1 cored and thinly sliced small apple

Directions:

1. Arrange the kale leaves onto a smooth surface.

2. Spread the cashew butter in the center of each kale leaf evenly.

3. Arrange 1 banana over buttered area of each leaf.

4. Place the apple slices around the bananas evenly.

5. Drizzle the fruit with agave nectar.

6. Wrap the kale leaves around the fruit tightly.

7. With a sharp knife, cut into desired sized sushi rolls and serve immediately.

WONDERFUL WAFFLE SUSHI ROLLS (4 SERVINGS, SERVING: 1 PORTION)

Per Serving, Calories: 318- Fat: 7.5g - Carbs: 50g - Protein: 13.5g

Ingredients:

- 1 cup of Bisquick baking mix

- ¼ cup of sugar

- 2 eggs

- 8-ounce of whipped cream cheese

- 1 cup of hulled and slices fresh strawberries

- ¼ cup of maple syrup

Directions:

1. Preheat the pizzelle maker.

2. In a bowl, add Bisquick mix, sugar and eggs and mix till well combined.

3. Add heaping tablespoons of dough onto the pizzelle maker and cook for about 30 seconds.

4. Repeat with remaining mixture.

5. Arrange the pizzelle onto a cutting board.

6. Spread the cream cheese over each pizzelle and top with strawberry slices.

7. Carefully wrap the pizzelle into a tube shape with the fillings in the center.

8. With a sharp knife, cut the tube into sushi rolls

9. Serve with the drizzling of maple syrup.

FUSION PANCAKE SUSHI ROLLS (4 SERVINGS, SERVING: 1 PORTION)

Per Serving, Calories: 933- Fat: 50.4g - Carbs: 93.2g - Protein: 27.1g

Ingredients:

- 4 (11-inch) Russian pancakes

- 3½-ounce of softened cream cheese

- 3½-ounce of chopped smoked salmon

- 4 tsp. of creamy horseradish sauce

- 1 peeled, pitted and sliced avocado

- ¼ cup of chopped fresh spinach

- Freshly ground black pepper, to taste

Directions:

1. Keep the pancakes aside to cool.

2. Place the pancakes onto a smooth surface.

3. Spread the cream cheese over the lower third of each pancake evenly.

4. Place the chopped salmon over cream cheese, followed by horseradish sauce, avocado slices and spinach.

5. Sprinkle with black pepper.

6. Roll the pancakes around the filling tightly.

7. With a sharp knife, cut into desired sized sushi rolls and serve immediately.

PERFECT CREPE SUSHI ROLLS (4 SERVINGS, SERVING: 1 PORTION)

Per Serving, Calories: 283- Fat: 8.2g - Carbs: 23.8g - Protein: 10g

Ingredients:

For Crepes:

- 1 cup of whole wheat flour

- 1 cup of milk

- 3 large eggs

- ¾ cup of water

- 1 tbsp. of unsalted butter

- 1 tbsp. of honey

- 1 tsp. of vanilla extract

- ¼ tsp. of salt

For Filling:

- 2 cored and chopped medium apples

- ½ tsp. of ground cinnamon

- ¼ cup of water

Directions:

1. For crepes in a blender, add all ingredients and pulse till smooth.

2. Heat a greased skillet on medium heat.

3. Add desired amount of mixture and tilt the pan to spread in the bottom evenly.

4. Cook for about 2 minutes or till golden brown.

5. Carefully, flip the side and cook for about 1 minute or till golden brown.

6. Remove from the heat and keep aside to cool.

7. Meanwhile for filling in a microwave safe dish, place the apples, cinnamon and water and microwave for about 5 minutes.

8. In a food processor, add the apple mixture and pulse just for a few seconds.

9. Arrange the crepe onto a smooth surface.

10. Spread the apple mixture over each crepe evenly and roll tightly.

11. With a sharp knife, cut into desired sized sushi rolls and serve immediately.

EXCELLENT CREPE SUSHI ROLLS (6 SERVINGS, SERVING: 1 PORTION)

Per Serving, Calories: 445- Fat: 17.9 g - Carbs: 67.7g - Protein: 9.2g

Ingredients:

- 1 cup of oat flour

- ½ cup of almond meal

- 1½ cups of unsweetened almond milk

- 2 tbsp. of honey

- 2 tbsp. of melted coconut oil, divided

- 1½ tsp. of vanilla extract

- 3 tbsp. of peanut butter

- 1½ cups of peeled, pitted and thinly sliced mango slices

Directions:

1. In a food processor, add flour, almond meal, almond milk, honey, 1 tbsp. of coconut oil and vanilla extract and pulse till smooth.

2. In a skillet, heat remaining coconut oil on medium heat.

3. Add desired amount of mixture and tilt the pan to spread in the bottom evenly.

4. Cook for about 2 minutes or till golden brown.

5. Carefully, flip the side and cook for about 1 minute or till golden brown.

6. Remove from heat and keep aside to cool. Arrange the crepe onto a smooth surface.

7. Spread peanut butter over each crepe evenly.

8. Place the mango slices over one end of each crepe and roll tightly.
9. With a sharp knife, cut into desired sized sushi rolls and serve immediately.

MORNING GLORY SUSHI ROLLS (2 SERVINGS, SERVING: 1 PORTION)

Per Serving, Calories: 103- Fat: 6.7g - Carbs: 2g - Protein: 9.7g

Ingredients:

- 3 eggs

- 1 tbsp. of milk

- Freshly ground pepper, to taste

- 1 tbsp. of peeled and finely chopped carrot

- 1 tbsp. of finely chopped onion

- 1 tbsp. of finely chopped scallion (green part)

- Salt, to taste

Directions:

1. In a bowl, add the eggs, milk and salt and beat till well combined.

2. Through a fine sieve, strain the egg mixture into another bowl.

3. Add carrot, onion, scallion and pepper and stir till well combined.

4. Heat a lightly greased frying pan on low heat.

5. Add ½ of the egg mixture and cook till half done.

6. Roll the omelet half way from the right to the middle.

7. And move the egg roll to the right edge of the pan.

8. Add ¼ egg mixture to cover the left half of the pan and cook till half done.

9. Roll again half way up from the right to the left and move the egg roll to the right side of the pan.

10. Add the remaining egg mixture and cook till half done.

11. Roll all the way up.

12. Transfer to a cutting board and keep aside to cool before cutting.

13. With a sharp knife, cut into desired sized sushi rolls and serve immediately.

ELEGANT SUSHI ROLLS (2 SERVINGS, SERVING: 1 PORTION)

Per Serving, Calories: 458- Fat: 32.8g - Carbs: 15.4g - Protein: 25.9g

Ingredients:

- 4 eggs, divided

- 1/3 cup of milk, divided

- ¼ cup of shredded Monetary Jack cheese, divided

- 2 warmed whole wheat flour tortillas

- 4 cooked bacon strips

- 1 peeled, pitted and sliced small avocado

- 1 sliced small tomato

Directions:

1. In a small bowl, add 2 eggs and 3 tablespoons of milk and beat till well combined.

2. Heat a greased medium skillet on medium-high heat.

3. Add the egg mixture in skillet and sprinkle with 2 tablespoons of the cheese.

4. Cook for about 3-5 minutes, without stirring.

5. Place the tortilla over the egg and gently flip onto a cutting board.

6. Place 2 bacon strips in the bottom of the tortilla and top with ½ of the avocado and tomato slices.

7. Roll the tortilla tightly.

8. Repeat with the remaining tortilla and other ingredients.

9. With a sharp knife, cut into desired sized sushi rolls and serve immediately.

DECADENT SUSHI ROLLS (1 SERVING, SERVING: 1 PORTION)

Per Serving, Calories: 351- Fat: 22g - Carbs: 28g - Protein: 13g

Ingredients:

- 1 large egg

- 3 tbsp. of liquid egg whites

- Salt and freshly ground black pepper, to taste

- 1 whole wheat tortilla

- 2 tbsp. of shredded cheese

- ½ of peeled, pitted and mashed avocado

- 1 cup of chopped fresh baby spinach

Directions:

1. In a small bowl, add egg, liquid egg whites, salt and black pepper and beat till well combined.

2. Heat a greased small skillet on medium-low heat.

3. Add the egg mixture and cook, covered for about 1-2 minutes.

4. Flip and cook for about 30 seconds.

5. Arrange the tortilla onto a smooth surface.

6. Sprinkle the tortilla with the cheese, leaving a 2-inch border around the edges.

7. Place egg in the center of the tortilla, followed by avocado and top spinach.

8. Roll the tortilla tightly.

9. Heat the same greased skillet on medium-high heat.

10. In the skillet, place the tortilla roll, seam-side down and cook till golden brown from both sides.

11. Remove from the heat and keep aside for about 1-2 minutes.

12. With a sharp knife, cut into desired sized sushi rolls and serve immediately.

Foolproof Sushi Rolls (1 serving, serving: 1 portion)

Per Serving, Calories: 330- Fat: 12.8g - Carbs: 37.9g - Protein: 18.8g

Ingredients:

- 3 beaten egg whites

- 1 whole wheat low-carb tortilla

- 1 tbsp. of prepared hummus

- 1 peeled and sliced into strips small carrot

- 3-4 cooked asparagus spears

- ¼ of peeled, pitted and sliced avocado

- Dash of Sriracha

Directions:

1. Heat a greased small non-stick skillet on medium heat.

2. Add egg whites and cook for about 3-5 minutes, without stirring.

3. Carefully, flip egg white crepe and cook for about 1-2 minutes.

4. Transfer the egg white crepe onto a cutting board.

5. Spread hummus across the tortilla evenly and top with carrot, asparagus and avocado slices.

6. Roll tortilla, tucking the veggies inside tightly.

7. With a sharp knife, cut into desired sized sushi rolls.

8. Drizzle with Sriracha and serve immediately.

SUNDAY MORNING SUSHI ROLLS (3 SERVINGS, SERVING: 1 PORTION)

Per Serving, Calories: 399- Fat: 17.1g - Carbs: 36.3g - Protein: 24.5g

Ingredients:

- 2 tbsp. of softened cream cheese

- 1 tbsp. of all-purpose flour

- Salt, to taste

- 1/3 cup of whole milk

- 6 large eggs

- 1 seeded and julienned red bell pepper

- 4 thin asparagus spears

- ½ cup of finely grated Parmesan cheese

- ½ cup of cooked rice

Direction:

1. Preheat the oven to 375 degrees F.

2. Line a 13x9-inch baking dish with a large greased parchment paper so that edges of paper are hanging over pan, forming a sling.

3. In a bowl, add cream cheese, flour and salt and beat till well combined.

4. Slowly, add milk and beat till smooth.

5. Add the eggs and beat till well combined.

6. Place the mixture into the prepared baking dish.

7. Bake for about 30-35 minutes or till eggs are set.

8. Meanwhile in a pan of boiling water, blanch bell pepper and asparagus till slightly softened but still firm.

9. Remove the baking dish from the oven.

10. With the parchment paper carefully, remove egg mixture from the baking dish and immediately, sprinkle with cheese.

11. Place the cooked rice on top of egg mixture, 1-inch from the edge of the long side and forming a rectangle about 2-inch wide.

12. Place bell pepper strips and asparagus spears next to rice, forming a line across the egg rectangle.

13. Roll up the egg mixture from large side to secure the filling.

14. Keep aside in room temperature for a few minutes to cool.

15. With a sharp knife, cut into desired sized sushi rolls and serve immediately.

Exotic Sushi Rolls (2 servings, serving: 1 portion)

Per Serving, Calories: 351- Fat: 28.7g - Carbs: 11.6g - Protein: 15.1g

Ingredients:

- ¼ cup of sliced turkey sausage

- ½ of cut into strips zucchini

- 2 large eggs

- 2 large egg whites

- 1 peeled, pitted and mashed avocado

- ¼ cup of broccoli

Directions:

1. Heat a medium skillet on medium-high heat

2. Add sausage and cook for about 6-8 minutes.

3. Drain the grease rom the skillet

4. In the same skillet, add zucchini and cook for about 2-3 minutes.

5. Remove from the heat and keep aside to cool slightly.

6. In a small bowl, add egg and egg whites and beat till well combined.

7. Heat a greased large skillet on medium-high heat.

8. Add the egg mixture and tilt the pan to spread the mixture in the bottom evenly.

9. Cook for about 1-2 minutes per side.

10. Carefully, transfer the egg crepe onto a smooth surface.

11. Spread the mashed avocado over the egg crepe evenly.

12. In a mini food processor, add the broccoli and pulse till a rice like consistency is formed.

13. Transfer the broccoli into a microwave safe bowl and microwave for about 1 minute.

14.

Sprinkle the broccoli rice over the mashed avocado, followed by zucchini and sausage.

15. Carefully, roll the crepe.

16. With a sharp knife, cut into desired sized sushi rolls and serve immediately.

Tastier Sushi Rolls (4 servings, serving: 1 portion)

Per Serving, Calories: 662- Fat: 47.6 g - Carbs: 19.6g - Protein: 38.1g

Ingredients:

- 2 cups of tater tots

- 1 seeded and finely chopped jalapeño pepper

- 2 eggs

- 10 bacon strips

- 1 cup of shredded cheddar cheese

Directions:

1. Preheat the oven to 375 degrees F.

2. In a bowl, mix together tater tots, jalapeño pepper and eggs.

3. Arrange a large piece of foil onto a smooth surface.

4. Make a bacon weave over the foil, so there are 5 strips lengthwise and 5 strips widthwise.

5. Secure each end with toothpicks to keep bacon from pulling apart.

6. Spread the egg mixture over the bacon weave evenly, leaving 1 (2-inch) end of bacon weave blank.

7. Sprinkle with the cheese evenly.

8. With the help of foil, wrap the sushi tightly and secure with toothpicks.

9. Arrange the roll onto a baking sheet and remove the foil.

10. Bake for about 45 minutes or till bacon is done completely.

11. Remove from the oven and keep aside for about 4-5 minutes.

12. With a sharp knife, cut into desired sized sushi rolls and serve immediately.

Luxurious Breakfast Sushi Rolls (4 servings, serving: 1 portion)

Per Serving, Calories: 594- Fat: 41.1g - Carbs: 21.7g - Protein: 33.9g

Ingredients:

- 30 pieces of tater tots

- 1 large egg

- 10 bacon strips

- ½ cup of shredded Swiss cheese

- 1 seeded and thinly sliced green bell pepper

Directions:

1. Preheat the oven to 350 degrees F.

2. In a bowl, add tater tots and egg and with a fork, mash till well combined.

3. Make a bacon weave onto a smooth surface, so there are 5 strips lengthwise and 5 strips widthwise.

4. Secure each end with toothpicks to keep bacon from pulling apart.

5. Spread the egg mixture across bacon weave evenly, leaving about a strip of bacon uncovered at the top.

6. Sprinkle with the cheese evenly.

7. Place the bell pepper slices over the cheese across.

8. Wrap the sushi tightly and secure with toothpicks.

9. Arrange the roll onto a baking sheet.

10. Bake for about 35-40 minutes or till bacon is done completely.

11. Remove from the oven and keep aside for about 4-5 minutes.

12. With a sharp knife, cut into desired sized sushi rolls and serve immediately.

FLAVORED SUSHI ROLLS (4 SERVINGS, SERVING: 1 PORTION)

Per Serving, Calories: 877- Fat: 65.6g - Carbs: 17.9g - Protein: 51.2g

Ingredients:

- 25 pieces of tater tots

- 12 bacon slices

- ½ pound of casing removed breakfast sausage

- 4 American cheese slices

- 2 scrambled eggs

Directions:

1. Preheat the oven to 400 degrees F. Arrange a wire rack onto a large baking sheet.

2. Cook tater tots according to package's directions.

3. Make a bacon weave onto a smooth surface, so there are 6 strips lengthwise and 6 strips widthwise.

4. Secure each end with toothpicks to keep bacon from pulling apart.

5. Place sausage in a 1-pound Ziploc bag and with a rolling pin, flatten into 9-inch of the length.

6. Cut off the zipper and then, cut down both sides of the bag, leaving the bottom seam attached.

7. Open the bag and place cheese slices over the sausage evenly, leaving 1-inch space at the top and ½-inch spaces on both sides.

8. Place the tater tots in a line along the bottom third.

9. Place the scrambled eggs next to the tater tots.

10. Pull 1 edge up and over the filling.

11. Pull it tightly to roll then keep rolling to the end.

12. Tuck in the sides.

13. Pick up the roll with the bag and gently place over the bottom edge of the bacon weave.

14. Pull up the bottom edge of the bacon's plastic wrap and roll forward to wrap the sausage.

15. Place the roll onto the prepared baking sheet.

16. Bake for about 30-40 minutes.

17. Remove from the oven and keep aside to cool for about 15 minutes.

18. With a sharp knife, cut into desired sized sushi rolls and serve immediately.

Sweetly Delish Sushi Rolls (23 servings, serving: 1 portion)

Per Serving, Calories: 514- Fat: 41.6g - Carbs: 66.5 Protein: 11.7g

Ingredients:

- 3½-ounce of rinsed sushi rice

- 1 (14-ounce) can of coconut milk

- 1 tbsp. of agave nectar

- ½ cup of granola

- ½ cup of peeled and sliced banana

Directions:

1. In a pan, add the coconut milk and agave nectar on very low heat ad cook for about 20 minutes, stirring continuously.

2. Grease a baking sheet with a parchment paper.

3. Place the cooked sushi onto the prepared baking sheet in an even layer and keep aside to cool slightly.

4. Arrange a sushi mat flat onto a smooth surface and place some cling film on top of it.

5. Sprinkle the granola over the cling film evenly.

6. Place the clumps of cooked rice over the granola and pat it down slightly on the sushi mat to smooth the surface.

7. Place the banana pieces in a line about 2/5ths of the way up the sushi.

8. Carefully, roll into cling film and refrigerate for at least 30 minutes.

9. With a sharp knife, cut into desired sized sushi rolls and serve immediately.

FAVORITE SUSHI ROLLS (6 SERVINGS, SERVING: 1 PORTION)

Per Serving, Calories: 287- Fat: 21.4g - Carbs: 3g - Protein: 19.5g

Ingredients:

- 8 center-cut bacon slices

- 1 can of crescent rolls

- 4 eggs

- Freshly ground black pepper, to taste

- ¼ cup of shredded cheddar cheese

Directions:

1. Preheat the oven to 400 degrees F. Line a baking sheet with a piece of foil and arrange rack over the foil.

2. Place the bacon strips over the rack in a single layer.

3. Bake for about 8-10 minutes.

4. Remove from the oven and keep aside to cool.

5. Now, reduce the temperature of oven to 350 degrees F. Lined another baking sheet with a parchment paper.

6. Roll out the crescent rolls and press the seams together.

7. Keep the rolls aside.

8. In a small bowl, beat the eggs.

9. Heat a greased nonstick skillet on medium heat.

10. Add the eggs and cook for about 2-3 minutes, stirring continuously.

11. Stir in black pepper and remove from the heat.

12. Keep aside to cool slightly.

13. Place the bacon slices side by side on the rolled out crescent roll, perpendicular to the long edge.

14. Sprinkle with the cheese evenly and top with the eggs.

15. Roll the crescent rolls, starting at the long edge of the crescents, begin rolling up the crescents evenly, ending with seam side-down.

16. Arrange the rolls onto the prepared baking sheet.

17. Bake for about 10 minutes.

18. Remove from the oven and keep aside for about 5 minutes.

19. With a sharp knife, cut into desired sized sushi rolls and serve immediately.

FRUITY BREAKFAST SUSHI ROLLS (10 SERVINGS, SERVING: 1 PORTION)

Per Serving, Calories: 161- Fat: 21.6g - Carbs: 25.7g - Protein: 2.9g

Ingredients:

- 10 dried rice paper wrappers

- 2 tbsp. of uncooked amaranth

- 2 tbsp. of uncooked barley

- 2 tbsp. of uncooked spelt

- ¾ cup of maple water

- 1 cup of pitted and chopped peach

- 1 cup of peeled and chopped kiwi

- 1 cup of peeled and sliced banana

- 3 tbsp. of coconut flakes

Directions:

1. In a small pan, add the amaranth, barley, spelt and maple water and bring to a boil.

2. Reduce heat to low and simmer for about 15-20 minutes or till all the liquid is absorbed.

3. Transfer the cooked grains into a bowl and keep aside to cool.

4. Soak the rice paper wrappers, one at a time in warm water for about 5 seconds or till soft.

5. Transfer the rice paper wrapper onto a cutting board.

6. In a bowl, mix together the chopped fruit.

7. Place chopped fruit in a line in the center of each wrapper, leaving about 1½-inch above and below.

8. Place the grains in a line to the right of the fruit and top with the coconut flakes.

9. Fold the top and bottom edges of the rice paper in and starting from the right roll to the left.

10. Carefully fold the right flap over the line of grains and coconut flakes.

11. Then fold all of that over the line of fruit and continue to roll to the left.

12. With a sharp knife, cut into desired sized sushi rolls and serve immediately.

WEEKEND SPECIAL SUSHI ROLLS (2 SERVINGS, SERVING: 1 PORTION)

Per Serving, Calories: 639- Fat: 21.8g - Carbs: 78.8g - Protein: 33.2g

Ingredients:

- 1 tbsp. of unsalted butter

- ½ of finely chopped yellow onion

- 1½ cups of chopped cooked potatoes

- ¾ cup of finely chopped corned beef

- 2 eggs

- 2¼ tsp. of sugar

- ½ tsp. of cornstarch

- Pinch of salt

- ½ tsp. of water

Directions:

1. In a large nonstick skillet, melt butter on medium-high heat.

2. Add onion and sauté for about 5 minutes.

3. Add potato and corned beef and stir to combine well.

4. With a spatula, press the mixture down to create a compact layer.

5. Reduce the heat to medium and cook for about 15 minutes.

6. Meanwhile for the crepes in a bowl, add the eggs and beat till frothy.

7. Whisk in sugar, cornstarch, salt and water and beat till well combined.

8. Heat a lightly greased 8-inch nonstick skillet on low heat.

9. Place half of the mixture and tilt the pan to coat the bottom evenly and cook for about 1 minute or till set.

10. Carefully, flip the side and cook for about 10 seconds.

11. Transfer the crepe onto a plate and keep aside to cool.

12. Repeat with the remaining mixture.

13. Line 2 (8x8-inch) bamboo sushi mats with plastic wraps.

14. Arrange 1 egg crepe over each prepared sushi mat.

15. Place ¼ cup of corned beef mixture in a line over the lower third of each crepe.

16. Pull the bottom of the mat up to roll the crepe over the filling.

17. Pull it tight and keep rolling to the end.

18. With a sharp knife, cut into desired sized sushi rolls and serve immediately.

AWESOME SUSHI ROLLS (1 SERVING, SERVING: 1 PORTION)

Per Serving, Calories: 369- Fat: 32.7g - Carbs: 8.7g - Protein: 13.8g

Ingredients:

- ½ tbsp. of sesame oil

- ½ tsp. of finely grated fresh ginger

- 2 eggs

- 2 tbsp. of almond milk

- 1 tbsp. of finely chopped fresh chives

- 1 tsp. of chili flakes

- Salt and freshly ground black pepper, to taste

- 1 cup of chopped fresh spinach

- ¼ of peeled, pitted and sliced avocado

Directions:

1. In a frying pan, heat the sesame oil on medium heat.

2. Add the grated ginger and sauté for about 30 seconds.

3. Meanwhile in a bowl, add the eggs, almond milk, chives, chili flakes, salt and black pepper and beat till well combined.

4. Place about half of the egg mixture and tilt the pan to cover the bottom and cook for about 2-3 minutes.

5. Top the egg mixture with half of the spinach evenly and cook till wilted.

6. Carefully, transfer the omelet onto a smooth surface.

7. Repeat with the remaining egg mixture and spinach.

8. Place a sheet of nori on top of each omelet so that it covers the surface of the omelet.

9. Place the avocado slices on the bottom quarter of each nori sheet and tightly roll the omelet into a sushi roll.

10. With a sharp knife, cut into desired sized sushi rolls and serve immediately.

FOOLPROOF SUSHI ROLLS (1 SERVING, SERVING: 1 PORTION)

Per Serving, Calories: 683- Fat: 10.5g - Carbs: 120.2g - Protein: 21.6g

Ingredients:

- 1 seaweed sheet

- 1 tbsp. of salsa

- ¼ cup of scrambled egg

- ¼ cup of cooked and sliced sausage

- ¼ cup of cooked and shredded home fries

Directions:

1. Arrange the seaweed sheet onto a smooth surface with the long side closest to you.

2. Gently spread a thin layer of salsa over the sheet evenly.

3. Place the scrambled egg over the sheet, 1-inch from the edge of the sheet, followed by sausage and fries.

4. Gently, fold seaweed sheet over filling, lightly pressing to form a roll. Continue rolling.

5. With a sharp knife, cut into desired sized sushi rolls and serve immediately.

NUTRITIVE SUSHI ROLLS (4 SERVINGS, SERVING: 1 PORTION)

Per Serving, Calories: 205- Fat: 7.6g - Carbs: 24.1g - Protein: 11.8g

Ingredients:

- 1 cup of scrambled egg

- 8 smoked salmon slices

- 1 tbsp. of minced fresh dill

- 1½ of peeled, pitted and sliced avocados

- 1 cup of torn fresh spinach

Directions:

1. Arrange 4 plastic wrap squares onto a smooth surface.

2. Arrange 1 nori sheet over each plastic square.

3. Place scrambled eggs over each sheet evenly.

4. Top with smoked salmon slices, followed by dill, avocado slices and spinach.

5. Carefully take the end of the nori and roll it over the ingredients using the plastic wrap.

6. With a sharp knife, cut into desired sized sushi rolls and serve immediately.

Yummy Sushi Rolls (4 servings, serving: 1 portion)

Per Serving, Calories: 205- Fat: 7.6g - Carbs: 24.1g - Protein: 11.8g

Ingredients:

- 4 ham slices

- 3 cups of steamed sushi rice

- 5 tbsp. of sushi seasoning

- 4 scrambled eggs

- 4 roasted fresh seaweed sheets

Directions:

1. Heat a frying pan of medium heat and fry the ham slices till desired doneness.

2. Cut each ham slices in half and keep aside.

3. Meanwhile in a bowl, add sushi rice and seasoning and mix well.

4. Batter 2 eggs at a time and fry the 2 battered eggs.

5. Arrange the seaweed sheets onto a smooth surface.

6. Place the rice over each seaweed sheet and flatten into a thick layer.

7. Place 2 halves ham slices onto each sheet over the ham slices.

8. Top with the eggs

9. Fold each sheet in half and then roll.

10. With a sharp knife, cut into desired sized sushi rolls and serve immediately.

AMERICAN STYLE SUSHI BAGELS (2 SERVINGS, SERVING: 1 PORTION)

Per Serving, Calories: 549- Fat: 20.5g - Carbs: 62.8g - Protein: 29.3g

Ingredients:

- 2 halved and toasted sesame seed bagels

- 2 tbsp. of softened cream cheese

- 1 tsp. of wasabi paste

- 1 sliced scallion

- 2 tsp. of chopped pickled ginger

- 6 smoked salmon slices

- 4 cucumber slices

- 2 scrambled eggs

Directions:

1. In a bowl, add cream cheese with wasabi paste and beat till well combined.

2. Stir in the scallion and pickled ginger.

3. Spread the cream cheese mixture over the bottom half of each bagels.

4. Top with the salmon, cucumber and scrambled eggs evenly.

5. Cover with the tops of the bagels.

FRUITY SUSHI BOWL (4 SERVINGS, SERVING: 1 BOWL)

Per Serving, Calories: 387- Fat: 0.7g - Carbs: 89.1g - Protein: 5.3g

Ingredients:

- 2 cups of water

- 1½ cups of rinsed sushi rice

- 2 tbsp. of rice vinegar

- 1½ tbsp. of granulated sugar

- Salt, to taste

- 1½ tbsp. of maple syrup

- ½ tsp. of ground cinnamon

- 1 cup of fresh blackberries

Directions:

1. In a small pan, add the sushi rice and water and bring to a boil.

2. Reduce the heat to low and simmer, covered for about 20 minutes.

3. Remove from the heat and keep aside, covered for about 10 minutes.

4. In a small microwave safe bowl, add rice vinegar, sugar and salt and microwave for about 20 seconds.

5. Remove from the microwave and stir till sugar is dissolved. Place the vinegar mixture over the sushi rice and mix well.

6. Divide the sushi rice into 3 bowls evenly. In a small bowl, mix together the maple syrup and cinnamon.

7. Drizzle the sushi rice bowls with the maple syrup mixture evenly and mix well.

8. Top with the black berries and serve.

SIMPLE BREAKFAST SUSHI BOWL (1 SERVING, SERVING: 1 BOWL)

Per Serving, Calories: 744- Fat: 5.6g - Carbs: 149.6g - Protein: 18.9g

Ingredients:

- 1 cup of cooked hot white rice

- ½ tsp. of soy sauce

- ½ tsp. of mirin

- Pinch of salt

- 1 poached egg

- Pinch of minced fresh chives

Directions:

1. In a bowl, add rice, soy sauce, mirin and salt and stir to combine.

2. Place the poached egg on top.

3. Sprinkle with chives and serve immediately.

CHAPTER 2: LUNCH RECIPES

EASIEST SUSHI ROLLS (4 SERVINGS, SERVING: 1 PORTION)

Per Serving, Calories: 484- Fat: 24.8g - Carbs: 58.5g - Protein: 7.5g

Ingredients:

- 2¼ cups of water

- 1½ cups of rinsed sushi rice

- 1 tbsp. of rice wine vinegar

- ½ tbsp. of sugar

- Pinch of salt

- 4 nori sheets

- 2 peeled, pitted and sliced large avocados

Directions:

1. In a pan, add water and rice and bring to a boil on high heat.

2. Reduce the heat to a medium and simmer, covered for about 20 minutes.

3. Meanwhile in microwave safe bowl, add vinegar, sugar and salt and microwave for about 10-15 seconds.

4. Transfer the rice into a large bowl.

5. Add the vinegar mixture and gently, stir to combine.

6. Keep aside in room temperature to cool completely.

7. Cover 4 bamboo mats with plastic wrap.

8. Arrange 1 nori sheet over each bamboo mat, shiny side down.

9. Place a thin layer of cooled rice over each sheet and press, leaving at least ½-inch top and bottom edge of the sheet uncovered.

10. Place avocado slices across the rice, leaving 1-inch of rice uncovered at the far edge.

11. Slightly wet the top edge of the sheet and roll from bottom to the top edge with the help of the bamboo mat tightly.

12. With a sharp knife, cut into desired sized sushi rolls and serve immediately.

VEGGIE TREAT SUSHI ROLLS (10 SERVINGS, SERVING: 1 PORTION)

Per Serving, Calories: 312- Fat: 6.2g - Carbs: 54.5g - Protein: 7.1g

Ingredients:

- 3 cups of rinsed short-grain Japanese rice

- 3¼ cups of water

- 1/3 cup of rice vinegar

- 3 tbsp. of sugar

- 1 tsp. of salt

- 10 nori sheets

- 3 tsp. of sesame seeds

- 1 torn romaine lettuce heart

- 1 peeled and cut into matchsticks cucumber

- 1 peeled, pitted and thinly sliced avocado

- 1 seeded and thinly sliced plum tomato

- 1 thinly sliced small red onion

- 20 trimmed and blanched asparagus spears

- 3 tbsp. of wasabi paste

Directions:

1. Prepare the rice in cook in a rice cooker with 2 cups of the water.

2. In a small pan, add the vinegar, sugar and salt on medium heat and cook till the sugar dissolves, stirring continuously.

3. Transfer the rice into a large bowl and immediately, stir in the vinegar mixture.

4. Keep aside for about 5 minutes.

5. Cover 4 bamboo mats with plastic wrap.

6. Arrange 1 nori sheet over each bamboo mat, shiny side down.

7. Place a thin layer of cooled rice over each sheet and press, leaving at least ½-inch top and bottom edge of the sheet uncovered.

8. Sprinkle with sesame seeds and spread a little wasabi paste on top.

9. Place lettuce, cucumber, avocado, tomato and onion in a tight pile in the lower third of the sheet.

10. Slightly wet the top edge of the sheet and roll from bottom to the top edge with the help of the bamboo mat tightly.

11. With a sharp knife, cut into desired sized sushi rolls and serve immediately.

ENTICING SUSHI ROLLS (4 SERVINGS, SERVING: 1 PORTION)

Per Serving, Calories: 356- Fat: 5.5g - Carbs: 67.4g - Protein: 7.4g

Ingredients:

- 1½ cups of water

- 1½ cups of rinsed sushi rice

- 1/3 cup of seasoned rice vinegar

- 2 tsp. of sugar

- 1 tsp. of salt

- 4 toasted nori sheets

- ½ of peeled, seeded and cut into matchsticks cucumber

- 1 peeled and cut into matchsticks carrot

- 1 seeded and cut into matchsticks small orange bell pepper

- 4 cut into matchsticks scallions

- 6 trimmed and cut into matchsticks red radishes

- ½ of peeled, pitted and thinly sliced Hass avocado

Directions:

1. In a medium pan, add water and rice on high heat and bring to a boil.

2. Reduce heat to very low and simmer, covered for about 15 minutes.

3. Meanwhile in a bowl, mix together vinegar, sugar and salt.

4. Remove the rice from the heat and keep aside, covered for about 10 minutes.

5. With a fork, fluff the rice and transfer into a large bowl.

6. Add the vinegar mixture and toss to coat well.

7. Spread the rice onto a parchment paper-lined baking sheet to cool completely.

8. Place 4 bamboo mats onto a smooth surface.

9. Arrange 1 nori sheet over each bamboo mat, shiny side down.

10. Place a thin layer of cooled rice over each sheet and press, leaving at least 1½-inch top and bottom edge of the sheet uncovered.

11. Place cucumber, carrot, bell pepper, scallion, radish and avocado across the rice, leaving 1-inch of rice uncovered at the far edge.

12. Slightly wet the top edge of the sheet and roll from bottom to the top edge with the help of the bamboo mat tightly.

13. With a sharp knife, cut into desired sized sushi rolls and serve immediately.

GREEK INSPIRED SUSHI ROLLS (2 SERVINGS, SERVING: 1 PORTION)

Per Serving, Calories: 505- Fat: 9.3g - Carbs: 85.4g - Protein: 13.3g

Ingredients:

- 3 cups of water

- 1 tsp. of salt

- 1 cup of rinsed sushi rice

- ¼ cup of rice vinegar

- 2 nori sheets

- 4-ounce of cut into thin strips roasted red peppers

- 10 pitted and halved kalamata olives

- 2-ounce of crumbled feta cheese

- 1 peeled and sliced into thin strips medium cucumber

Directions:

1. In a medium pan, add the water and salt on medium heat and bring to a boil.

2. Add rice and again bring to a boil.

3. Reduce heat to low and simmer, covered till the water is absorbed.

4. Remove from the heat and stir in the rice vinegar.

5. Keep aside to cool completely.

6. Place 2 bamboo mats onto a smooth surface.

7. Arrange 1 nori sheet over each bamboo mat, shiny-side down.

8. Place a thin layer of cooled rice over each sheet and press, leaving at least 1½-inch top and bottom edge of the sheet uncovered.

9. Place the roasted red peppers, olives, feta, and cucumber horizontally across the rice.

10. Slightly wet the top edge of the sheet and roll from bottom to the top edge with the help of the bamboo mat tightly.

11. With a sharp knife, cut into desired sized sushi rolls and serve immediately.

FAVORITE SUSHI ROLLS (4 SERVINGS, SERVING: 1 PORTION)

Per Serving, Calories: 319- Fat: 11g - Carbs: 45.2g - Protein: 8.8g

Ingredients:

- 1½ cups of water

- 1 cup of rinsed sushi rice

- ¼ cup of seasoned rice vinegar

- 4 nori sheets

- 1 peeled, pitted and cut into thin slices avocado

- 1 peeled and cut into thin slices carrot

- ½ of peeled and cut into thin slices cucumber

- ½ cup of faux chicken strips

Directions:

In a pan, add water and rice and bring to a boil. Reduce the heat and simmer, covered for about 15-20 minutes.

Remove from the heat and keep aside, covered for about 10 minutes. Add the seasoned rice vinegar and keep in the room temperature to cool completely.

Place 4 bamboo mats onto a smooth surface. Arrange 1 nori sheet over each bamboo mat, shiny-side down.

Place a thin layer of cooled rice over each sheet and press, leaving at least 1½-inch top and bottom edge of the sheet uncovered.

Place the carrot, cucumber, avocado and faux chicken strips horizontally across the rice.

Slightly wet the top edge of the sheet and roll from bottom to the top edge with the help of the bamboo mat tightly.

With a sharp knife, cut into desired sized sushi rolls and serve immediately.

WESTERN STYLE SUSHI ROLLS (4 SERVINGS, SERVING: 1 PORTION)

Per Serving, Calories: 382- Fat: 10g - Carbs: 65.3g - Protein: 4.2g

Ingredients:

- 1½ cups of water

- 1½ cups of rinsed short-grain white rice

- 1/3 cup of red wine vinegar

- 2 tsp. of white sugar

- 1 tsp. of salt

- ½ of peeled, pitted and thinly sliced avocado

- 1 tsp. of fresh lemon juice

- ¼ cup of sesame seeds

- ½ of peeled, seeded and cut into matchsticks green bell pepper

- ½ of peeled, seeded and cut into matchsticks cucumber

- ½ of cut into matchsticks zucchini

Directions:

1. In a pan, add water and rice and bring to a boil on high heat.

2. Reduce the heat to very low and simmer, covered for about 15 minutes.

3. Remove from the heat and keep aside, covered for about 10 minutes.

4. Meanwhile in a bowl, mix together the vinegar, sugar, and salt.

5. With a fork, fluff the rice and transfer into a large bowl.

6. Add the vinegar mixture into the rice and stir to combine.

7. Spread rice out onto a large baking sheet and keep in the room temperature to cool completely.

8. In a bowl, add avocado slices and drizzle with lemon juice.

9. Arrange 4 bamboo mats onto a smooth surface.

10. Sprinkle each mat with a thin layer of sesame seeds.

11. Place cooled rice onto each bamboo mat in an even layer.

12. Place cucumber, avocado slices, bell pepper and zucchini in a line down the middle of the rice.

13. Pick up the edge of the bamboo mat, fold the bottom edge of the sheet up, enclosing the filling.

14. Roll tightly into a thick cylinder.

15. With a sharp knife, cut into desired sized sushi rolls and serve immediately.

COLORED SUSHI ROLLS (6 SERVINGS, SERVING: 1 PORTION)

Per Serving, Calories: 134- Fat: 1.7g - Carbs: 23.2g - Protein: 4.3g

Ingredients:

- 2 cups of water

- 2 cups of rinsed sushi rice

- ¼ cup of rice vinegar

- 2 tbsp. of cane sugar

- 1 tsp. of salt

- 6 nori sheets

- 2 tbsp. of black sesame seeds

- 1 peeled and cut into matchsticks small orange carrot

- 1 peeled and cut into matchsticks small purple carrot

- 12 trimmed and blanched asparagus spears

- ½ of seeded and cut into matchsticks English cucumber

- ½ of cut into matchsticks yellow squash

Directions:

1. In a pan, add water and rice on medium-high heat and bring to a boil.

2. Reduce the heat to low and simmer, covered till all the liquid is absorbed.

3. Remove from the heat and keep aside, covered for about 10-15 minutes.

4. Meanwhile in a bowl, mix together the vinegar, sugar, and salt.

5. With a fork, luff the rice and transfer into a large bowl.

6. Add the vinegar mixture into the rice and stir to combine.

7. Keep aside to cool completely.

8. Arrange 6 bamboo mats onto a smooth surface.

9. Arrange 1 nori sheet over each bamboo mat, shiny-side down.

10. Sprinkle with sesame seeds.

11. Place a thin layer of cooled rice over each sheet and press, leaving at least 1½-inch top and bottom edge of the sheet uncovered.

12. Place carrot, asparagus, cucumber and squash in a pile horizontally along the lower third of the wrap.

13. Pick up the edge of the bamboo mat, fold the bottom edge of the sheet up, enclosing the filling.

14. With a sharp knife, cut into desired sized sushi rolls and serve immediately.

BEST SUSHI ROLLS (2 SERVINGS, SERVING: 1 PORTION)

Per Serving, Calories: 431- Fat: 7.1g - Carbs: 60.2g - Protein: 7.6g

Ingredients:

- ¾ cup of water

- 2/3 cup of rinsed sushi rice

- ½ tbsp. of rice vinegar

- ½ tsp. of salt

- 2 tbsp. of vegetable oil

- 1 minced garlic clove

- 2 tbsp. of chili paste

- ½ of sliced into thin strips medium eggplant

- 1 sliced scallion

- 2 nori sheets

- ½ tsp. of sesame seeds

Directions:

1. In a pan, add water, rice, vinegar and salt and bring to a boil.

2. Reduce the heat to very low and simmer, covered for about 20 minutes.

3. Remove from the heat and keep aside, covered for about 10 minutes.

4. Meanwhile in a medium skillet, heat on medium heat.

5. Add garlic and chili paste and sauté for about 1 minute.

6. Place the eggplant in a single layer and cook for about 5 minutes per side.

7. Remove from the heat and keep aside to cool slightly.

8. Arrange 2 bamboo mats onto a smooth surface.

9. Arrange 1 nori sheet over each bamboo mat, shiny-side down.

10. Place a thin layer of cooled rice over each sheet and press, leaving at least 1½-inch top and bottom edge of the sheet uncovered.

11. Place the eggplant in a single line horizontally across the rice.

12. Place the scallion, slices alongside the eggplant.

13. Sprinkle with the sesame seeds.

14. Slightly wet the top edge of the sheet and roll from bottom to the top edge with the help of the bamboo mat tightly.

15. With a sharp knife, cut into desired sized sushi rolls and serve immediately.

Delish Sushi Rolls (6 servings, serving: 1 portion)

Per Serving, Calories: 331- Fat: 9.1g - Carbs: 52.4g - Protein: 10.7g

Ingredients:

- 5 cups of water

- 2 cups of rinsed wild rice mix

- 2 tbsp. of maple syrup

- 2 tbsp. of rice vinegar

- 1 tsp. of ground cinnamon

- 2 peeled and cut into thin strips lengthwise baked sweet potatoes

- 1 peeled, pitted and cut into thin strips lengthwise avocado

- ¼ cup of sliced almonds

- 6 nori sheets

Directions:

1. In a rice cooker, place the water and wild rice mix and cook on Brown Rice setting.

2. Transfer cooked rice to a bowl and stir in maple syrup, vinegar and cinnamon.

3. Keep aside to cool completely.

4. Arrange 6 bamboo mats onto a smooth surface.

5. Arrange 1 nori sheet over each bamboo mat, shiny-side down.

6. Place a thin layer of cooled rice over each sheet and press, leaving at least 1½-inch top and bottom edge of the sheet uncovered.

7. Place the sweet potato slices horizontally across the rice.

8. Top with thin rows of avocado and sliced almonds.

9. Slightly wet the top edge of the sheet and roll from bottom to the top edge with the help of the bamboo mat tightly.

10. With a sharp knife, cut into desired sized sushi rolls and serve immediately.

COLORFUL SUSHI ROLLS (2 SERVINGS, SERVING: 1 PORTION)

Per Serving, Calories: 484- Fat: 22.6g - Carbs: 62.4g - Protein: 10.6g

Ingredients:

- 1¼ pound of sweet potatoes

- 1/3 cup of almond milk

- 3 tbsp. of white miso

- Freshly ground black pepper, to taste

- 16-ounce of trimmed and chopped fresh kale

- 1 peeled, pitted and chopped small avocado

- 2 tbsp. of olive oil

- 2 tbsp. of fresh lemon juice

- ½ tsp. of salt

- 2 nori sheets

- 1 cup of kimchee

Directions:

1. Preheat the oven to 400 degrees F.

2. With a fork, prick each sweet potato a few times.

3. Arrange the sweet potatoes onto a baking sheet.

4. Bake for about 35-45 minutes.

5. Remove from the oven and keep aside to cool slightly.

6. Cut each sweet potato in half and scoop out the flesh.

7. In a food processor, add the sweet potatoes, almond milk, miso and black pepper and pulse till smooth.

8. In a large bowl, add the kale, avocado, oil, lemon juice and salt.

9. With your hands, massage the ingredients into the kale till time kale is creamy and wilted.

10. Arrange 2 bamboo mats onto a smooth surface.

11. Arrange 1 nori sheet over each bamboo mat, shiny-side down.

12. Spread about ½ cup of the sweet potato mash over each nori sheet, a few inches above the bottom of the sheet and end a few inches below the top of the sheet.

13. Place a layer of kale salad on top and make a horizontal strip of kimchee in the center.

14. Slightly wet the top edge of the sheet and roll from bottom to the top edge with the help of the bamboo mat tightly.

15. With a sharp knife, cut into desired sized sushi rolls and serve immediately.

Super-Tasty Sushi Rolls (2 servings, serving: 1 portion)

Per Serving, Calories: 720- Fat: 13g - Carbs: 128.3g - Protein: 19.7g

Ingredients:

- 1½ cups of cooked sushi rice

- 1 cut into quarters in lengthwise English cucumber

- 1 tbsp. of vegetable oil

- 3 trimmed and finely chopped asparagus stalks

- ½ of seeded and finely chopped red bell pepper

- 4 finely chopped white buttons mushrooms

- 2 finely chopped scallions

- 2 nori sheets

- 1 tbsp. of soy sauce

- 1 tbsp. of Sriracha sauce

- 1 tbsp. of rice vinegar

Directions:

1. With a teaspoon, scoop out the seeds and inside of each cucumber piece till hollow.

2. In a pan, heat the oil on medium-high heat.

3. Add the vegetables and cook for about 3-4 minutes.

4. Remove from the heat and stir in the soy sauce and Sriracha.

5. Add rice and vinegar and with a wooden spoon gently, stir to combine.

6. Transfer the mixture into a bowl and keep aside in room temperature to cool completely.

7. Arrange the nori sheets onto a smooth surface.

8. Spread the rice mixture over each nori sheet from top to bottom evenly.

9. Carefully take the end of the nori and roll it over the ingredients using the plastic wrap.

10. With a sharp knife, cut into desired sized sushi rolls and serve immediately.

Decent Sushi Rolls (2 servings, serving: 1 portion)

Per Serving, Calories: 884- Fat: 15.3g - Carbs: 169.6g - Protein: 17.1g

Ingredients:

- 2 cups of cooked brown rice

- 1 tbsp. of brown rice vinegar

- 1 tsp. of mirin

- ½ tsp. of salt

- 2 nori sheets

- ½ cup of kimchee

- ½ of peeled, pitted and sliced into thin strips mango

- ½ of peeled, pitted and sliced into thin strips avocado

- ¼ of seeded and thinly sliced into strips red bell pepper

Directions:

1. In a large bowl, mix together the cooked rice, vinegar, mirin and salt.

2. Cover 2 bamboo mats with plastic wrap.

3. Arrange 1 nori sheet over each bamboo mat, shiny side down.

4. Place a thin layer of cooled rice over each sheet and press, leaving at least ½-inch top and bottom edge of the sheet uncovered.

5. Place mango, avocado, bell pepper and kimchee across the rice, leaving 1-inch of rice uncovered at the far edge.

6. Slightly wet the top edge of the sheet and roll from bottom to the top edge with the help of the bamboo mat tightly.

7. With a sharp knife, cut into desired sized sushi rolls and serve immediately.

Superb Sushi Rolls (2 servings, serving: 1 portion)

Per Serving, Calories: 286- Fat: 0.8g - Carbs: 61.5g - Protein: 6.3g

Ingredients:

- ¾ cup plus 2 tbsp. of water

- 2/3 cup of rinsed sushi rice

- ½ tbsp. of rice vinegar

- 1 tsp. of salt

- ½ of seeded and sliced into thin strips green bell pepper

- ½ of peeled, pitted and sliced into thin strips ripe mango

- 1 thinly sliced scallion

- 2 nori sheets

Directions:

1. In a pan, add water, rice, vinegar and salt and bring to a boil.

2. Reduce the heat to very low and simmer, covered for about 20 minutes.

3. Remove from the heat and keep aside, covered for about 10 minutes.

4. Arrange 2 bamboo mats onto a smooth surface.

5. Arrange each nori sheet over each bamboo mat, shiny-side down.

6. Place a thin layer of rice over each sheet and press, leaving at least 1½-inch top and bottom edge of the sheet uncovered.

7. Arrange mango in a single line along the width of wrapper, about 1-inch from edge.

8. Arrange half of bell pepper strips alongside the mango, then half of scallion slices alongside that.

9. Slightly wet the top edge of the sheet and roll from bottom to the top edge with the help of the bamboo mat tightly.

10. With a sharp knife, cut into desired sized sushi rolls and serve immediately.

Mexican Style Sushi Rolls (6 servings, serving: 1 portion)

Per Serving, Calories: 641- Fat: 36g - Carbs: 65g - Protein: 19.7g

Ingredients:

For Rice:

- 1 tbsp. of olive oil

- ½ of finely chopped yellow onion

- 2 minced garlic cloves

- 2 cups of rinsed brown rice

- 2 cups of vegetable broth

- 1 cup of water

- 1 (14-ounce) can of unsalted tomato sauce

- 2 tbsp. of canned green chiles

- 1 tsp. of ground cumin

- ½ cup of chopped fresh cilantro

- 2 tbsp. of tomato paste

- 2 tbsp. of fresh lime juice

- Salt and freshly ground black pepper, to taste

For Taco Meat:

- 2 cups of walnuts

- ¼ cup of sun-dried tomatoes

- 2 tbsp. of coconut aminos

- 1 tsp. of ground cumin

- 1 tsp. of ancho chile powder

- ½ tsp. of smoked paprika

- Salt and freshly ground black pepper, to taste

- 6 nori sheets

- 1 peeled, pitted and thinly sliced avocado

- 1 seeded and thinly sliced bell pepper

Directions:

1. In a large skillet, heat the olive oil on medium heat.

2. Add onion and garlic and sauté for about 4-5 minutes.

3. Add rice and sauté for about 1-2 minutes.

4. Add the broth, water, tomato sauce, green chiles and cumin and bring to a boil.

5. Reduce the heat to low and simmer, covered till the liquid is absorbed, stirring occasionally.

6. Stir in the cilantro, tomato paste, lime juice, salt and black pepper and remove from the heat.

7. Transfer the rice into a bowl and keep aside in room temperature to cool completely.

8. Meanwhile for the taco meat in a fid processor, add all ingredients and pulse till chopped into small pieces.

9. Transfer into a bowl and keep aside.

10. Wrap 6 bamboo mat with plastic wraps and arrange onto a smooth surface.

11. Arrange 1 nori sheet over each bamboo mat, shiny side down.

12. Place a thin layer of cooled rice over each sheet and press, leaving at least ½-inch top and bottom edge of the sheet uncovered.

13. Make a line of taco meat from left to right about 1-inch from the edge.

14. Top with a line of bell pepper and avocado slices.

15. Slightly wet the top edge of the sheet and roll from bottom to the top edge with the help of the bamboo mat tightly.

16. With a sharp knife, cut into desired sized sushi rolls and serve immediately.

VEGAN SUSHI ROLLS (6 SERVINGS, SERVING: 1 PORTION)

Per Serving, Calories: 107- Fat: 5.4g - Carbs: 3.5g - Protein: 8g

Ingredients:

- 10-ounce of drained and pressed sprouted super firm tofu

- 1 roughly chopped scallion

- 4 tbsp. of rice vinegar

- 2 tsp. of sesame oil

- ½ tsp. of salt

- ¼ tsp. of garlic powder

- 6 nori sheets

- 1 peeled and cut matchstick slices large carrot

- ½ of peeled and cut matchstick slices English cucumber

Directions:

1. In a food processor, add the tofu, scallion, vinegar, sesame oil, salt and garlic powder and pulse till the tofu is chopped into tiny pieces.

2. Arrange 6 bamboo mats onto a smooth surface.

3. Arrange 1 nori sheet over each bamboo mat, shiny-side down.

4. Spread some of the tofu mixture over each nori sheet about 1/3-½ of the sheet full.

5. Place carrots and cucumber on top of the tofu.

6. Slightly wet the top edge of the sheet and roll from bottom to the top edge with the help of the bamboo mat tightly.

7. With a sharp knife, cut into desired sized sushi rolls and serve immediately.

SUPERB SUSHI ROLLS (4 SERVINGS, SERVING: 1 PORTION)

Per Serving, Calories: 242- Fat: 15g - Carbs: 17.8g - Protein: 12.4g

Ingredients:

- 4 nori sheets

- 1 pound thinly sliced cucumbers

- 1 tsp. of sesame seeds

- 1/8 tsp. of red chili powder

- 1 peeled, pitted and sliced avocado

- 3½-ounce of cut into strips cooked tofu

- ½ of peeled and cut into strips jicama

Directions:

1. Arrange the nori sheets onto a smooth surface, shiny side down.

2. Arrange the cucumber slices in overlapping rows onto each nori sheet from the left edge to right edge, leaving 1-inch margin uncovered at right.

3. Sprinkle with sesame seeds and chili powder.

4. Arrange avocado slices, tofu and jicama slices in an even vertical pattern, 2-inch from the left edge.

5. Roll the nori sheet tightly by folding the edges over the filling and stick with the wet fingers.

6. With a sharp knife, cut into desired sized sushi rolls and serve immediately.

HEALTHY LUNCHEON SUSHI ROLLS (4 SERVINGS, SERVING: 1 PORTION)

Per Serving, Calories: 294- Fat: 12.5g - Carbs: 35.7g - Protein: 8.7g

Ingredients:

- 2 cups of water

- 1 cup of quinoa

- 3 tbsp. of brown rice vinegar

- 1 tsp. of maple syrup

- Pinch of salt

- 4 nori sheets

- 1 cup of chopped fresh spinach

- 1 peeled and thinly sliced small cucumber

- 1 peeled, pitted and thinly sliced avocado

Directions:

1. In a pan, add quinoa and water and bring to a boil.

2. Reduce heat and simmer till all the liquid is absorbed.

3. Meanwhile in a small bowl, mix together vinegar, maple syrup and salt.

4. Transfer the cooked quinoa onto a large plate.

5. Slowly, add the vinegar mixture on quinoa and mix till well combined.

6. Arrange 1 nori sheet over each bamboo mat, shiny side down.

7. Place a thin layer of quinoa over each sheet and press, leaving at least 1½-inch top and bottom edge of the sheet uncovered.

8. Place the spinach, cucumber and avocado horizontally across the quinoa.

9. Slightly wet the top edge of the sheet and roll from bottom to the top edge with the help of the bamboo mat tightly.

10. With a sharp knife, cut into desired sized sushi rolls and serve immediately.

PROTEIN LOADED SUSHI ROLLS (4 SERVINGS, SERVING: 1 PORTION)

Per Serving, Calories: 245- Fat: 7.6g - Carbs: 35.6g - Protein: 7.8g

Ingredients:

- 2 cups of water

- 1 cup of quinoa

- 1 tsp. of ground ginger

- ¼ tsp. of salt

- 1 tbsp. of agave nectar

- 1 tbsp. of rice vinegar

- 4 nori sheets

- ½ of peeled, pitted and thinly sliced avocado

- ½ of peeled and thinly sliced medium cucumber

- ½ of peeled and cut into thin strips baby carrots

- 1 cup of torn romaine lettuce

Directions:

1. In a rice cooker, add water, quinoa, ground ginger and salt.

2. Close the lid and cook on White Rice setting.

3. Remove from the heat and transfer into a bowl.

4. Stir in agave nectar and vinegar and keep aside to cool completely.

5. Arrange 1 nori sheet over each bamboo mat, shiny side down.

6. Place a thin layer of quinoa over each sheet and press, leaving at least 1½-inch top and bottom edge of the sheet uncovered.

7. Place the avocado, cucumber, carrots and lettuce horizontally across the quinoa.

8. Slightly wet the top edge of the sheet and roll from bottom to the top edge with the help of the bamboo mat tightly.

9. With a sharp knife, cut into desired sized sushi rolls and serve immediately.

GREAT SUSHI ROLLS (4 SERVINGS, SERVING: 1 PORTION)

Per Serving, Calories: 431- Fat: 32.9g - Carbs: 5g - Protein: 27.4g

Ingredients:

- 10 bacon slices

- 2 tbsp. of mayonnaise

- 1 cup of chopped tomatoes

- 1 cup of shredded romaine lettuce

- Salt and freshly ground black pepper, to taste

Directions:

1. Preheat the oven to 400 degrees F. Arrange a wire rack onto a large baking sheet.

2. Make a bacon weave onto the prepared baking sheet, so there are 5 strips lengthwise and 5 strips widthwise.

3. Secure each end with toothpicks to keep bacon from pulling apart.

4. Bake for about 20 minutes.

5. With the paper towels, pat dry the bacon weave to drain the fat.

6. Transfer the weave onto a plastic wrap piece.

7. Spread a thin layer of mayonnaise over bacon weave evenly.

8. Place the tomatoes over the bottom 1/3 of the weave, followed by lettuce.

9. Sprinkle with salt and pepper.

10. Wrap the sushi tightly and secure with toothpicks.

11. With a sharp knife, cut into desired sized sushi rolls and serve immediately.

EASIEST SUSHI ROLLS (8 SERVINGS, SERVING: 1 PORTION)

Per Serving, Calories: 562- Fat: 42.7g - Carbs: 27.7g - Protein: 19.2g

Ingredients:

- 4 peeled, pitted and sliced small avocados

- 1 tbsp. of fresh lime juice

- Salt, to taste

- 8 egg roll wrappers

- 4 halved pepper jack cheese slices

- 10 cooked bacon slices

- ¼ cup of olive oil

Directions:

In a bowl, add avocado slices and drizzle with lime.

Sprinkle with salt and toss to coat well. Arrange 1 egg roll wrapper onto a smooth surface.

Place ½ of a cheese slice in the middle of wrapper, followed by 1 avocado slice, 1 bacon slice and 1 avocado slice.

Carefully fold the bottom of the wrapper over the filling.

Turn in the sides and continue rolling up from the bottom. Repeat with the remaining rolls and ingredients.

In a large frying pan, heat oil on medium heat and fry the egg rolls in batches golden brown from both sides.

Transfer onto a paper towel lined plate to drain.

Keep aside to cool slightly. With a sharp knife, cut into desired sized sushi rolls and serve immediately.

BARBECUE FLAVORED SUSHI ROLLS (2 SERVINGS, SERVING: 1 PORTION)

Per Serving, Calories: 616- Fat: 19.4g - Carbs: 88.9g - Protein: 16.2g

Ingredients:

- 1 cup of water

- 1 cup of rinsed sushi rice

- 1 tbsp. of rice vinegar

- 1 all-beef hot dog

- 1 nori sheet

- 1 tbsp. of chopped red onion

- ¼ cup of barbeque sauce, divided

- ¼ cup of shredded Cheddar cheese, divided

- 2 tbsp. of French-fried onions

Directions:

1. In a pan, add water, rice, vinegar and salt and bring to a boil.

2. Reduce the heat to very low and simmer, covered for about 15 minutes.

3. Remove from the heat and keep aside, covered for about 10 minutes.

4. Stir in the vinegar and keep aside to cool completely.

5. In a small pan of boiling water to a boil, add the hot dog and simmer for about 5 minutes.

6. Place a large piece of plastic wrap onto a smooth surface.

7. Arrange the nori sheet over the plastic wrap.

8. With wet fingers, spread cooled rice in an even layer over the nori sheet.

9. Place hot dog 1-inch from the bottom edge of rice and nori sheet.

10. Arrange the onion in a row beside the hot dog.

11. Spread 2 tbsp. of the barbeque sauce on top of the hot dog and sprinkle with 2 tbsp. of Cheddar cheese.

12. Carefully take the end of the nori and roll it over the ingredients using the plastic wrap.

13. With a sharp knife, cut into desired sized sushi rolls.

14. Top with remaining barbecue sauce and cheese and serve immediately.

Vietnamese Inspired Sushi Rolls (10 servings, serving: 1 portion)

Per Serving, Calories: 127- Fat: 4.5g - Carbs: 16.3g - Protein: 5.6g

Ingredients:

- 10 rice paper wrappers

- 3-ounce of cooked rice noodles

- 1 cup of torn lettuce leaves

- 1 cup of shredded purple cabbage

- 1 cup of peeled and julienned carrots

- 1 cup of peeled and julienned cucumbers

- 1 cup of chopped fresh cilantro

- 1 peeled, pitted and thinly sliced large avocado

- 30 cooked medium shrimp

- 1 tbsp. of sesame seeds

Directions:

1. In a shallow baking dish, place about 1½ cups of warm water.

2. Dip the rice paper wrapper, one at a time in the warm water for about 10-15 seconds.

3. Arrange the rice papers onto a smooth surface.

4. Place a small amount of rice noodles in a pile over one third of each rice paper.

5. Top with lettuce leaves, cabbage, carrots, cucumbers and cilantro.

6. Arrange the avocados slices next to the rice noodles and 3 shrimp placed in a row next to the avocados.

7. Sprinkle with the sesame seeds.

8. Carefully fold the bottom of the rice paper wrapper over the filling and turn in the sides and continue rolling up from the bottom.

9. With a sharp knife, cut into desired sized sushi rolls and serve immediately.

Favorite Lunchtime Sushi Rolls (6 servings, serving: 1 portion)

Per Serving, Calories: 937- Fat: 18.5g - Carbs: 114.3g - Protein: 28.7g

Ingredients:

- 4½-ounce of softened light cream cheese

- 1½ tsp. of wasabi paste

- 3 tbsp. of chopped scallion

- 6 nori sheets

- 4½ cups of cooked sushi rice

- 12-ounce of thinly sliced smoked salmon

Directions:

In a bowl, add cream cheese, wasabi paste and scallion and mix till well combined.

Cut the top quarter of each nori sheet along short end.

Place 1 nori sheet, shiny side down, over a bamboo mat covered with plastic wrap, with long end toward you.

Place ¾ cup of the rice over each nori sheet and with moist hands press them, leaving a 1-inch border on one long end of nori.

Gently flip the nori sheet. Spread 1½ tbsp. of cream cheese mixture over top third of shiny side of nori and top with 1/3 cup of the salmon.

Lift edge of nori closest to you and fold over the filling.

Lift bottom edge of the bamboo mat and roll toward top edge, pressing firmly on sushi roll.

Roll to top edge and press mat to seal the sushi roll.

With a sharp knife, cut into desired sized sushi rolls and serve immediately.

NUTRIENT-RICH SUSHI ROLLS (4 SERVINGS, SERVING: 1 PORTION)

Per Serving, Calories: 570- Fat: 14.2g - Carbs: 81.3g - Protein: 24.7g

Ingredients:

- 3¾ cups of water

- 2 cups of rinsed sushi rice

- Salt, to taste

- 3 tbsp. of rice vinegar

- 1 tbsp. of sugar

- 4-ounce of softened cream cheese

- 2 chopped scallions

- 2 peeled and finely chopped carrots

- 12-ounce of thinly sliced smoked salmon

Directions:

1. In a pan, add water, rice and salt and bring to a boil.

2. Reduce the heat to low and cook, covered for about 15 minutes, without stirring.

3. Remove the pan from the heat and keep, covered for about 15 minutes.

4. Transfer the rice to a baking sheet.

5. Add the vinegar and sugar and stir to combine.

6. Keep aside to cool for about 10-20 minutes.

7. In a bowl, mix together the cream cheese, scallion and carrots.

8. Arrange 4 lightly greased plastic wrap pieces onto a smooth surface.

9. Place rice on each plastic wrap piece evenly and w wet hands, press into a 7-inch square.

10. Place the salmon over the rice, leaving a ½-inch border on the side.

11. Place the cream cheese mixture along the edge of salmon slices.

12. With the plastic wrap, roll the sushi up into a cylinder.

13. Press the rice together with even pressure to form a roll.

14. Repeat with the remaining ingredients, making 3 more rolls.

15. With a sharp knife, cut into desired sized sushi rolls and serve immediately.

AUTHENTIC SUSHI ROLLS (6 SERVINGS, SERVING: 1 PORTION)

Per Serving, Calories: 202- Fat: 9.8g - Carbs: 17.5g - Protein: 10.2g

Ingredients:

- 2 cups of soaked for 4 hours and drained Japanese sushi rice

- 2 cups of water

- 1/3 cup of rice wine vinegar

- 6 nori sheets

- 1 peeled, pitted and sliced avocado

- 1 peeled and sliced cucumber

- 8-ounce of cut into long strips smoked salmon

- 2 tbsp. of wasabi paste

Directions:

1. Prepare the rice in cook in a rice cooker with 2 cups of the water.

2. Transfer the rice into a bowl and immediately, stir in the rice vinegar.

3. Keep aside to completely.

4. Arrange each nori sheet over 1 bamboo mat.

5. Place a thin layer of cooled rice over each sheet and press, leaving at least ½-inch top and bottom edge of the sheet uncovered.

6. Top with the wasabi in the form of dots.

7. Arrange cucumber, avocado and smoked salmon over the rice about 1-inch away from the bottom edge of the sheet.

8. Slightly wet the top edge of the seaweed and roll from bottom to the top edge with the help of the bamboo mat tightly.

9. With a sharp knife, cut into desired sized sushi rolls and serve immediately.

Nutty Sushi Bowl (4 servings, serving: 1 bowl)

Per Serving, Calories: 270- Fat: 13.5g - Carbs: 4.2g - Protein: 31.8g

Ingredients:

- ½ of julienned sweet onion

- 1 chopped scallion

- 1 (1-inch) piece of finely grated fresh ginger

- 2 minced garlic cloves

- ¼ cup of soy sauce

- ½ tbsp. of sambal oelek

- 1 tsp. of sesame oil

- 1 pound of cut into ½-inch chunks ahi tuna

- 2 tbsp. of toasted and chopped macadamia nuts

Directions:

1. In a bowl, mix together onion, scallion, ginger, garlic, soy sauce, sambal oelek and sesame oil.

2. Add the tuna and toss to coat well.

3. Refrigerate for about 30 minutes before serving.

4. Stir in the macadamia nuts and serve.

LIGHTER SUSHI BOWL (3 SERVINGS, SERVING: 1 BOWL)

Per Serving, Calories: 322- Fat: 21.9g – Carbs: 12.5g – Protein: 22.7g

Ingredients:

- ½ pound of finely chopped ahi tuna

- 1 peeled, pitted and chopped avocado

- 1 chopped cucumber

- 2 tbsp. of chopped scallion

- 1 tbsp. of soy sauce

- 2 tsp. of mirin

- 1 tsp. of Sriracha

- ½ tsp. of toasted sesame oil

- 2 tsp. of toasted black sesame seeds

Directions:

1. In a large bowl, add all ingredients except sesame seeds and mix well.

2. Top with sesame seeds and serve.

Veggie Delight Sushi Bowl (3 servings, serving: 1 bowl)

Per Serving, Calories: 474- Fat: 9.3g – Carbs: 87.5g – Protein: 10.3g

Ingredients:

- 1½ cups of warm cooked brown rice
- 2 tbsp. of rice vinegar
- 1 tsp. of agave nectar
- Pinch of salt
- 1 toasted and cut into short strips nori sheet
- ½ of peeled, pitted and chopped medium avocado
- 1 peeled and cut into matchsticks medium carrot
- ½ of cut into matchsticks cucumber
- ½ cup of thinly sliced cooked shiitake mushroom caps
- ½ cup of peeled daikon radish
- 6 trimmed, cut into 2-inch lengths and blanched asparagus spears

Directions:

1. In a bowl, add the rice, vinegar, sugar and salt and mix till well combined.
2. Divide the rice into 3 serving bowls.
3. Top with remaining ingredients and serve.

Flavorsome Sushi Bowl (4 servings, serving: 1 bowl)

Per Serving, Calories: 572- Fat: 28.9g – Carbs: 72.1g – Protein: 8.4g

Ingredients:

For Sushi Bowl:

- 1 cup of rinsed white rice
- 2 cups of peeled and cut into 1-inch pieces sweet potatoes
- ½ tsp. of olive oil
- ¼ tsp. of salt
- 1/8 tsp. of freshly ground black pepper
- 1 peeled, pitted and chopped avocado
- 1 cup of cut into matchsticks cucumber
- 1 cup of cut into matchsticks carrot
- 2 toasted and cut into short strips nori sheets
- 1 tbsp. of toasted sesame seeds

For Dressing:

- 1 minced garlic clove
- 1½ tsp. of finely grated fresh ginger
- 3 tbsp. of water
- 3 tbsp. of tamari
- 2 tsp. of rice wine vinegar
- 2 tsp. of honey
- 1/8 tsp. of hot sauce

- 1/3 cup of olive oil

Directions:

1. Preheat the oven to 375 degrees F.

2. Cook the rice according to package's directions.

3. In a large baking sheet, place the chopped sweet potato, oil, salt and pepper and toss to coat well.

4. Roast for about 30-35 minutes.

5. For dressing in a small bowl, add all ingredients except oil and beat till well combined.

6. Slowly, add olive oil and beat till well combined.

7. In 4 serving bowls, divide rice, roasted sweet potatoes, avocado, cucumber, carrot and seaweed strips.

8. Drizzle with dressing and sprinkle with sesame seeds.

9. Serve immediately.

Unique Sushi Bowl (2 servings, serving: 1 bowl)

Per Serving, Calories: 930- Fat: 7.6g – Carbs: 81.6g – Protein: 10.1g

Ingredients:

For Rice:

- 1½ cups of water

- 1 cup of rinsed white rice

- ½ tbsp. of brown rice vinegar

- 1 tsp. of sugar

- 1 tsp. of salt

For Sushi Bowl:

- 20 ounces of drained, rinsed and cored canned unripe jack fruit in brine

- 1 tsp. of olive oil

- 2 ½ tbsp. of teriyaki sauce

- ¼ cup of water

- Salt, to taste

- 1 tsp. of vegetable oil

- 2 cups of fresh spinach

- 1 toasted and cut into short strips nori sheet

- 1 tbsp. of toasted sesame seeds

Directions

1. In a pan, add water and rice on medium-high heat and bring to a boil.

2. Reduce the heat to medium and cook, covered till all the liquid is absorbed.

3. Transfer the rice into a bowl and keep aside to cool completely.

4. After cooling, add the vinegar, sugar and salt and mix well.

5. In a pan, add the jackfruit and stir fry for about 4 minutes.

6. Stir in ½ tbsp. of teriyaki sauce and simmer, covered for about 15 minutes.

7. With 2 forks, shred the jackfruits completely.

8. Add remaining teriyaki sauce and salt and mix well.

9. Cook for about 1 minute.

10. Meanwhile in a frying pan, heat oil on medium heat.

11. Add spinach and cook for about 2-3 minutes.

12. Stir in salt and remove from the heat.

13. In 2 serving bowls, divide rice evenly.

14. Top with jackfruit mixture, spinach and nori strips.

15. Sprinkle with sesame seeds and serve,

CHAPTER 3: DINNER RECIPES

ENTRÉE SUSHI BOWL (3 SERVINGS, SERVING: 1 BOWL)

Per Serving, Calories: 531- Fat: 22.3g - Carbs: 73g - Protein: 12.9g

Ingredients:

- 2 cups of water

- 1 cup of rinsed short grain brown rice

- 1 green tea bag

- 2 tbsp. of rice vinegar

- 1 tbsp. of honey

- ¼ tsp. of salt

- ½ cup of peeled and thinly sliced carrots

- ½ cup of thinly sliced cucumbers

- ¼ cup thinly sliced radishes

- 2 tsp. of toasted sesame oil

- 2 tsp. of toasted black sesame seeds

- 1 peeled, pitted and chopped small avocado

- ½ cup of edamame

- ½ cup of seeded and thinly sliced red bell pepper

- 3 tbsp. of pickled ginger

Directions:

In a medium pan, add water, rice and green tea bag and stir to combine.

Cook, covered for about 45 minutes.

Remove from the heat and keep aside, covered for about 10 minutes.

Meanwhile in small bowl, add vinegar, honey and salt and beat till well combined.

Transfer the rice into a large bowl.

Add vinegar mixture and stir to combine.

In another bowl, mix together the carrot, cucumbers, radishes, sesame oil and sesame seeds.

Divide the rice into serving bowls.

Top with carrot mixture, avocado, edamame, bell pepper and scallion and serve.

Outrageous Sushi Bowl (4 servings, serving: 1 bowl)

Per Serving, Calories: 896- Fat: 32.3g - Carbs: 133.6g - Protein: 26.1g

Ingredients:

For Salad:

- 2 cups of water

- 1 cup of rinsed sushi rice

- 1 tbsp. of rice vinegar

- 2 cut into strips nori sheets

- 4-ounce of julienned cucumber

- 6-ounces of julienned daikon radish

- 6-ounce of peeled, pitted, and thinly sliced mango

- 1 cup of peeled, pitted, and thinly sliced avocado

- 1 cup of steamed and shelled edamame

- 3 tbsp. of toasted panko bread crumbs

- 1 tbsp. of toasted sesame seeds

For Sauce:

- 12-ounce of soft silken tofu

- ¼ cup of toasted sesame oil

- ¼ cup of rice vinegar

- 3 tbsp. of Sriracha

- ½ tsp. of salt

- ¼ tsp. of garlic powder

- ½ tsp. of agave nectar

Directions:

1. In a pan, add water, rice and vinegar and bring to a boil.

2. Reduce the heat to low and simmer for about 20-25 minutes.

3. Remove from heat and fluff with a fork.

4. Keep aside to cool slightly.

5. Meanwhile for sauce in a food processor, add all ingredients and pulse till smooth.

6. In a small bowl, mix together breadcrumbs and sesame seeds.

7. In serving bowl, divide the rice evenly.

8. Top with nori sheets, cucumber, radish, mango, avocado and edamame.

9. Drizzle with sauce and sprinkle with breadcrumbs mixture.

10. Serve immediately.

Richly-Flavored Sushi Bowl (4 servings, serving: 1 bowl)

Per Serving, Calories: 667- Fat: 28.1g - Carbs: 79.3g - Protein: 33.3g

Ingredients:

For Tofu:

- 1 (15-ounce) block of drained and pressed extra firm tofu

- 3 tbsp. of low-sodium soy sauce

- 1 tsp. of toasted sesame oil

- 1 minced garlic clove

- 1 tsp. of minced fresh ginger

For Salad:

- 1½ cups of vegetable broth

- 1 cup of uncooked quinoa

- 1½ cups of thawed and warmed frozen shelled edamame

- 1 cup of thinly sliced Napa cabbage

- 2 peeled, pitted and thinly sliced mangoes

- 1 peeled, pitted and thinly sliced avocado

- 2 toasted and crumbled nori sheets

- 2 chopped scallions

For Dressing:

- 1/3 cup of low-sodium soy sauce

- 3 tbsp. of fresh orange juice

- 3 tbsp. of mirin

- 2 tsp. of toasted sesame oil

- 1 minced garlic clove

- 1 tbsp. of minced fresh ginger

Directions:

1. With paper towels, pat dry the tofu and cut into 8 slices.

2. In the bottom of a small baking dish, mix together soy sauce, sesame oil, garlic and ginger.

3. Add the tofu strips and coat with the mixture evenly.

4. Keep aside for about 30 minutes, flipping once after 15 minutes.

5. Preheat the oven to 400 degrees F.

6. Arrange the marinated tofu strips onto a baking sheet and bake for about 20-25 minutes, flipping once in the middle way.

7. Meanwhile in a bowl, mix together broth and quinoa and bring to a boil.

8. Simmer for about 12-15 minutes.

9. Meanwhile for dressing in a bowl, add all ingredients and beat till well combined.

10. Remove the quinoa from the heat and transfer into a bowl.

11. Add half of dressing and stir to combine.

12. In serving bowls, divide the quinoa.

13. Top with edamame, cabbage, mango and avocado slices.

14. Sprinkle with scallion, nori and sesame seeds.

15. Drizzle with the remaining dressing and serve.

Veggie Burrito Sushi Bowl (3 servings, serving: 1 bowl)

Per Serving, Calories: 833- Fat: 37.1g - Carbs: 93.5g - Protein: 38.5g

Ingredients:

For Salad:

- 1¼ cups of water

- 1 cup of rinsed brown rice

- ½ tsp. of granulated garlic

- ½ tsp. of ground cumin

- ½ tsp. of red chile powder

- ½ tsp. of salt

- 1½ cups of rinsed and drained canned black beans

- ½ of seeded thinly sliced yellow bell pepper

- ½ of seeded thinly sliced red bell pepper

- 1 chopped tomato

- ½ of peeled, pitted and sliced avocado

- ½ cup of chopped jicama

- 2 cups of torn lettuce

For Sauce:

- 14-ounce of silken tofu

- 1 bunch of fresh cilantro

- 1 chopped small jalapeño pepper

- 1 chopped garlic clove

- ¼ cup of fresh lime juice

- Salt and freshly ground black pepper, to taste

Directions:

1. In a pan, add water, rice, spices and salt and bring to a boil.

2. Reduce the heat to low and simmer till all the liquid is absorbed.

3. Meanwhile for sauce in a food processor, add all ingredients and pulse till smooth.

4. Remove the rice from heat and immediately, stir in beans.

5. In the bottom of serving bowls, place the lettuce.

6. Top with rice mixture and vegetables.

7. Drizzle with sauce and serve.

WHOLESOME SUSHI BOWL (4 SERVINGS, SERVING: 1 BOWL)

Per Serving, Calories: 833- Fat: 37.1g - Carbs: 93.5g - Protein: 38.5g

Ingredients:

For Tempeh:

- 1 minced garlic clove

- 3 tbsp. of tamari

- 1 tbsp. of olive oil

- 1 tbsp. of sesame oil

- 9-ounce of cut into strips tempeh

For Dressing:

- ¼ cup of tahini

- 3 tbsp. of fresh lemon juice

- 3 tbsp. of water

- ¼ tsp. of garlic powder

- ¼ tsp. of salt

For Salad:

- 1 large peeled and cubed sweet potato

- 3 tbsp. of olive oil, divided

- 2 cups trimmed and chopped kale

- Salt, to taste

- ½ pound of sliced cremini mushrooms

- Freshly ground black pepper, to taste

- 1½ cups of cooked quinoa

- 1 cup of rinsed and drained canned black beans

- 2 tbsp. of chopped fresh cilantro

Directions:

For tempeh in a glass baking dish, mix together the garlic, tamari, olive oil and sesame oil.

Place the tempeh strips and coat with the mixture evenly.

Keep aside for about 30-40 minutes, flipping once in the middle way.

Preheat the oven to 375 degrees F. Line a baking sheet with parchment paper.

Transfer the tempeh strips onto the prepared baking sheet and bake for about 10-15 minutes per side.

For dressing in a bowl, add all ingredients and beat till well combined.

Refrigerate till serving. For sweet potato, preheat the oven to 375 degrees F. Line a baking sheet with parchment paper.

Arrange the sweet potato cubes onto the prepared baking sheet and drizzle with 1 tbsp. of oil.

Bake for about 35 minutes, flipping once in the middle way.

Meanwhile in a skillet, heat 1 tbsp. of olive oil on medium heat.

Add the kale and sauté for about 4-5 minutes.

Stir in pinch of salt and remove from heat.

In another skillet, heat remaining olive oil on medium heat and cook the mushrooms for about 6-7 minutes.

Stir in salt and black pepper and remove from heat.

In serving bowls, divide quinoa, black beans, tempeh, kale, sweet potato and mushrooms.

Drizzle with the dressing and garnish with cilantro. Serve immediately.

GOURMET SUSHI BOWL (4 SERVINGS, SERVING: 1 BOWL)

Per Serving, Calories: 556- Fat: 10.6g - Carbs: 78.4g - Protein: 33.7g

Ingredients:

- 1¼ pound of trimmed and thinly sliced chicken thigh fillets

- ¾ cup of teriyaki marinade

- 1½ cups of water

- 1½ cups of rinsed sushi rice

- 1½ tbsp. of mirin

- 2 tsp. of peanut oil

- 1 peeled and thinly sliced large carrot

- 1 thinly sliced Lebanese cucumber

- ¼ cup of pickled ginger

Directions:

1. In a bowl, add chicken strips and marinade and coat well.

2. Refrigerate to marinate for about 1 hour.

3. In a pan, add water and rice on medium-high heat and bring to a boil.

4. Reduce the heat to low and simmer, covered for about 12 minutes.

5. Remove from heat and keep aside, covered for about 10 minutes.

6. With a fork, fluff the rice.

7. Add mirin and gently stir to combine.

8. Keep aside to cool completely.

9. In a large frying pan, heat peanut oil on high heat.

10. Add chicken in 2 batches and sear for about 5-7 minutes or till done completely.

11. Transfer the chicken into a plate.

12. In serving bowls, divide rice and top with chicken, cucumber and pickled ginger.

13. Serve immediately.

Fiesta Sushi Bowl (4 servings, serving: 1 bowl)

Per Serving, Calories: 762- Fat: 31.4g - Carbs: 90.5g - Protein: 30.3g

Ingredients:

For Salad:

- 3 (4-ounce) skinless, boneless chicken breasts

- Salt and freshly ground black pepper, to taste

- 2 cups of warm cooked brown rice

- 2 peeled, pitted and thinly sliced avocados

- 2 peeled and thinly sliced carrots

- 2 toasted and thinly sliced nori sheets

- ¼ tsp. f chili flakes

- 1 tbsp. of toasted sesame seeds

For Miso Sauce:

- 1 cup of water

- 2 tbsp. of white miso

- 2 tbsp. of rice vinegar

- 1 tbsp. of cornstarch

- 1 tbsp. of coconut oil

- 1 tsp. of sesame oil

- 1 tsp. of honey

- ¼ tsp. of ground ginger

- 1 minced garlic clove

Directions:

1. Preheat the oven to 400 degrees F. Grease a baking sheet.

2. Season the chicken breasts with salt and black pepper evenly.

3. Arrange the chicken breasts onto prepared baking sheet in a single layer and bake for about 15-20 minutes.

4. Remove from the oven and keep aside for about 5 minutes.

5. Cut the chicken breasts into thin slices.

6. Meanwhile for sauce in a pan, mix together all ingredients on medium-low heat and bring to a boil, beating continuously.

7. Cook for about 30-40 seconds or till desired thickness, beating continuously.

8. Remove from heat and keep aside to cool slightly.

9. In serving bowls, divide rice, chicken, avocado, carrot and nori slices.

10. Sprinkle with chili flakes and sesame seeds and serve.

ENERGIZING SUSHI BOWL (4 SERVINGS, SERVING: 1 PORTION)

Per Serving, Calories: 871- Fat: 21,8g - Carbs: 135.7g - Protein: 35.1g

Ingredients:

For Salad:

- 1 peeled and cut into ½-inch cubes large sweet potato

- 1 chopped large red onion

- 3 tbsp. of olive oil, divided

- Salt and freshly ground black pepper, to taste

- 1 pound of skinless, boneless chicken breasts

- ½ tsp. of ground ginger

- ½ tsp. of garlic powder

- 4 cups of cooked brown rice

- 1 peeled, pitted and thinly slice avocado

- 2 cups of fresh baby spinach

- 2 tbsp. of chopped fresh cilantro

For Sauce:

- 1 minced garlic clove

- 1 tbsp. of soy sauce

- 2 tbsp. of smooth peanut butter

- 1 tbsp. of honey

- ¼ cup of fresh lime juice

- 1 tbsp. of olive oil

- 1 tbsp. of sesame oil

Directions:

a. Preheat the oven to 425 degrees F.

b. Place the sweet potatoes and red onions onto a large baking sheet in a single layer.

c. Add 1 tablespoon of olive oil, salt and pepper and toss to coat.

d. Bake for about 20-25 minutes.

e. Meanwhile season with garlic powder, ground ginger, salt, pepper evenly.

f. In a large skillet, heat 1 tbsp. of olive oil on medium heat.

g. Add chicken and cook for about 6-8 minutes per side.

h. Remove from heat and keep aside for about 10 minutes.

i. Cut each breast into 1-inch pieces.

j. For sauce in a bowl, add all ingredients and beat till smooth.

k. In serving bowls, divide rice and top with sweet potatoes, chicken, avocado and baby spinach.

l. Drizzle with sauce and sprinkle with cilantro.

m. Serve immediately.

KOREAN INSPIRED SUSHI BOWL (4 SERVINGS, SERVING: 1 BOWL)

Per Serving, Calories: 656- Fat: 15.2g - Carbs: 83.1g - Protein: 43.3g

Ingredients:

- 2 cup of rinsed sushi rice

- 1 minced garlic clove

- 1 tsp. of minced fresh ginger

- 2 tbsp. of soy sauce

- 1 tsp. of sesame oil

- 1 tbsp. of brown sugar

- 1 pound of lean ground beef

- 1½ tbsp. of vegetable oil

- ½ of chopped onion

- 1 peeled and cut into matchsticks large carrot

- 1 chopped large zucchini

- 2 cups of fresh baby spinach

- 1 tbsp. of toasted sesame seeds

Directions:

1. Cook the rice according to package's directions.

2. For the beef in a large bowl, mix together the garlic, ginger, soy sauce, sesame oil and brown sugar.

3. Add beef and coat with mixture generously.

4. Keep aside for about 15-20 minutes.

5. In a large skillet, heat oil on medium heat.

6. Add onion and sauté for about 2-3 minutes.

7. Stir in the beef and increase the heat to high.

8. Stir fry for about 3-4 minutes.

9. Add in the carrots, zucchini and cook for about 1-2 minute.

10. Add spinach and cook for about 2 minutes.

11. In serving bowls, divide the rice and top with beef mixture evenly.

12. Sprinkle with sesame seeds and serve.

NUTRITIOUS SUSHI BOWL (4 SERVINGS, SERVING: 1 BOWL)

Per Serving, Calories: 669- Fat: 10.6g - Carbs: 107.9g - Protein: 33.4g

Ingredients:

For Beef:

- 1 minced garlic clove

- 1 tbsp. of finely grated fresh ginger

- 1 cup of water

- ¼ cup of soy sauce

- 5 tbsp. of brown sugar

- 2 tbsp. of honey

- 2 tbsp. of corn flour

- ¼ cup of cold water

- 1 tbsp. of olive oil

- 4 (4-ounce) beef minute steaks

For Salad:

- 2 cups of cooked sushi rice

- 1 seeded and cut into thin strips yellow bell pepper

- 2 cups of peeled and grated carrot

- 2 cups of torn lettuce

- 1 tbsp. of toasted sesame seeds

Directions:

1. In a small bowl, dissolve the corn flour into cold water. Keep aside.

2. In a pan, add garlic, ginger, water, soy sauce, brown sugar and honey on high and bring to the boil, stirring continuously.

3. Reduce the heat to low and simmer for about 1-2 minutes.

4. Add 2 tbsp. of the hot sauce into the bowl of corn flour mixture and stir to combine.

5. Increase the heat to medium.

6. Add the corn flour mixture in the pan, beating continuously.

7. Remove from the heat and keep aside for about 5 minutes.

8. In a glass bowl, add ¾ of the sauce and reserve the remaining in another bowl.

9. Add beef steaks and coat with sauce generously.

10. Refrigerate for at least 30 minutes.

11. In a skillet, heat oil on high heat.

12. Add beef steaks and cook for about for 1 minute per side or till desired doneness.

13. Remove from the heat and keep aside for about 2-3 minutes.

14. Cut each steak into desired sized strips.

15. In serving bowls, divide rice and top with vegetables and steak strips.

16. Drizzle with reserve sauce and sprinkle with sesame seeds.

17. Serve immediately.

OMEGA-3 RICH SUSHI BOWL (2 SERVINGS, SERVING: 1 BOWL)

Per Serving, Calories: 772- Fat: 40.3g - Carbs: 69.5g - Protein: 36.9g

Ingredients:

For Dressing:

- 2 tbsp. of fresh lemon juice

- 2 tbsp. of apple cider vinegar

- 1 tbsp. of toasted sesame oil

- Pinch of salt

For Salad:

- 3 cups of shredded Napa cabbage

- 1 cup of cooked quinoa

- 1 scrambled egg

- 6-ounce of chopped cooked salmon

- 2 cups of fresh baby spinach

- 1 cup of thinly sliced radishes

- 1 peeled, pitted and thinly sliced avocado

- 1 toasted and crumbled nori sheet

- 1 tsp. of toasted black sesame seeds

Directions:

In a small bowl, add all dressing ingredients and beat till well combined.

1. In serving bowls, divide cabbage and top with remaining ingredients except sesame seeds.

2. Drizzle with dressing evenly.

3. Sprinkle with sesame seeds and serve.

STRENGTHENING SUSHI BOWL (2 SERVINGS, SERVING: 1 BOWL)

Per Serving, Calories: 760- Fat: 29.4g - Carbs: 92.3g - Protein: 30.6g

Ingredients:

For Salad:

- 1 cup of sushi rice

- 1 peeled, pitted and sliced avocado

- ½ cup of peeled and thinly sliced carrot

- ½ cup of thinly sliced cucumber

- ¼ cup of thinly sliced scallion

- 3-ounce of cooked and chopped salmon

- 3-ounce of cooked and chopped tuna

- 2 tbsp. of minced chives

- 1 tsp. of sesame seeds

For Dressing:

- 3 tbsp. of soy sauce

- 2 tbsp. of rice vinegar

- 1 tsp. of honey

- 1 tsp. of sesame oil

Directions:

1. Prepare the sushi rice according to package's directions.

2. Remove from the heat and cool slightly.

3. Meanwhile for dressing in a small bowl, add all ingredients and beat till well combined.

4. In serving bowls, divide rice.

5. Top with vegetables, salmon and tuna.

6. Drizzle with dressing and sprinkle with chives and sesame seeds.

7. Serve immediately.

Refreshingly Tasty Sushi Bowl (2 servings, serving: 1 bowl)

Per Serving, Calories: 732- Fat: 25.7g - Carbs: 91.5g - Protein: 28.1g

Ingredients:

For Salad:

- 1 cup of cooked sushi rice

- 1½ tbsp. of rice vinegar

- ¼ tsp. of salt

- 6-ounce of drained and fluffed canned salmon

- 1 peeled, pitted and thinly sliced avocado

- 1 thinly sliced cucumber

- 1 toasted and crumbled nori sheet

For Dressing:

- 3 tbsp. of soy sauce

- 1 tbsp. of fresh lemon juice

- 1 tbsp. of Sriracha

Directions:

1. In a bowl, mix together the cooked rice with rice vinegar and salt.

2. Divide the rice between two bowls for serving.

3. Top with salmon, avocado, cucumber and nori sheet to the two bowls.

4. For dressing in a bowl, mix together all ingredients.

5. Drizzle with the dressing and sprinkle with the sesame seed.

6. Serve immediately.

Sweet & Sour Sushi Bowl (4 servings, serving: 1 portion)

Per Serving, Calories: 428- Fat: 18.8g - Carbs: 32.1g - Protein: 33.1g

Ingredients:

For Dressing:

- 1 can of cream of coconut

- 2 tbsp. of tamari

- 1 tbsp. of rice wine vinegar

- ½ cup of chopped pineapple

- ½ of chopped red onion

- 1 tbsp. of minced red chile

- 1 tbsp. of minced green chile

- 1 minced garlic clove

- 2 tsp. of minced fresh ginger

- 2 tbsp. of fresh lemon juice

- Salt and freshly ground black pepper, to taste

For Salad:

- 1 pound of chopped cooked red snapper

- 2 thinly sliced scallions

- 2 tbsp. of chopped fresh mint leaves

- 2 tbsp. of chopped fresh cilantro

- ½ cup of shredded unsweetened coconut

- ¼ cup toasted macadamia nuts

Directions:

1. In a large bowl, add all dressing ingredients and mix well.

2. Add the snapper and toss to coat well.

3. Top with remaining ingredients and serve.

SURPRISINGLY TASTY SUSHI BOWL (6 SERVINGS, SERVING: 1 BOWL)

Per Serving, Calories: 629- Fat: 35.7g - Carbs: 46g - Protein: 32.8g

Ingredients:

For Tuna:

- 1 pound of ahi tuna steaks

- Salt and freshly ground black pepper, to taste

- 1½ tbsp. of sesame oil

- 3 tbsp. of mayonnaise

- 1½ tbsp. of chopped scallion

- 1 tbsp. of Sriracha

- ½ tsp. of fresh lemon juice

For Salad:

- 1½ cups of quinoa

- 2 tbsp. of coconut oil

- 1½ tsp. of minced fresh ginger

- 2 minced garlic cloves

- 6½ cups of trimmed and chopped fresh kale

- 1 tsp. of soy sauce

- 3 tsp. of fresh lemon juice

- Salt and freshly ground black pepper, to taste

- 2 peeled, pitted and thinly sliced avocados

- 2 peeled and cut into matchsticks medium carrots

- 1 cut into matchsticks medium cucumber

- 2 chopped scallions

- 2 tsp. of sesame seeds

For Vinaigrette:

- 1 minced garlic clove

- 1 tsp. of minced fresh ginger

- ¼ cup of sesame oil

- 2 tbsp. of soy sauce

- 1 tbsp. of rice vinegar

- 1 tbsp. of pineapple juice

- 1 tsp. of fresh lemon juice

- 1 tsp. of tahini

- ½ tsp. of Sriracha

Directions:

1. Season the tuna steaks with salt and pepper.

2. In a skillet, add sesame oil and tuna steaks on medium-high heat and sear for about 45 seconds per side.

3. Remove from the heat and keep aside to cool completely.

4. After cooling, chop the tuna steaks into ½-inch cubes.

5. In a bowl, mix together the mayonnaise, scallion, Sriracha and lemon juice.

6. Add tuna cubes and stir to combine well.

7. Refrigerator to chill before serving.

8. Meanwhile, cook the quinoa according to package's directions.

9. In a large skillet, melt coconut oil on medium heat.

10. Add ginger and garlic and sauté for about 1 minute.

11. Add kale and cook for about 4 minutes, stirring occasionally.

12. Add soy sauce and cook for about 4 minutes.

13. Remove from the heat and transfer into a large bowl.

14. Add cooked quinoa, lemon juice, salt and black pepper and mix well.

15. For vinaigrette in a small bowl, add all ingredients and beat till well combined.

16. In serving bowls, divide the quinoa evenly.

17. Top with tuna, carrots, cucumbers, and avocado and drizzle with vinaigrette.

18. Garnish with scallion and sesame seeds and serve.

Irresistible Sushi Bowl (2 servings, serving: 1 bowl)

Per Serving, Calories: 903- Fat: 39.1g - Carbs: 100.1g - Protein: 35.4g

Ingredients:

- 1 cup of cooked short grain rice

- 2 tbsp. of rice wine vinegar

- 8-ounce of cooked shrimp

- 1 tbsp. of extra-virgin olive oil

- Salt, to taste

- 1 peeled and sliced into matchsticks large carrot

- 1 peeled, pitted and thinly sliced avocado

- 1 cup of chopped cucumber

- ¼ cup of mayonnaise

- 2 tbsp. of Sriracha

- 2 tbsp. of fresh lemon juice

Directions:

1. In a bowl, add rice, vinegar and salt and toss to coat.

2. In another bowl, add shrimp, olive oil and salt and toss to coat.

3. In serving bowls, divide rice evenly.

4. Top with shrimp, carrot, avocado and cucumber.

5. In a small bowl, add remaining ingredients and stir to combine well.

6. Place mayonnaise mixture over shrimp mixture in each bowl and serve.

ENTICING SUSHI BOWL (4 SERVINGS, SERVING: 1 BOWL)

Per Serving, Calories: 553- Fat: 17.4g - Carbs: 88.2g - Protein: 17.4g

Ingredients:

- 2 cups of rinsed sushi rice

- 2 cups of rinsed sushi rice

- 5 tbsp. of rice vinegar, divided

- 1 tbsp. of sugar

- ½ tsp. of salt

- 1 peeled, pitted and sliced avocado

- 1 cup of chopped cucumber

- ½ cup of peeled and grated carrot

- 8-ounce of lump crabmeat

- 3 tbsp. of low-sodium soy sauce

- 2 tbsp. of chopped pickled ginger

- 2 tbsp. of toasted sesame seeds

Directions:

a. In a medium pan, add water and rice and bring to a boil.

b. Reduce the heat to low and simmer, covered for about 15 minutes.

c. Remove from heat and keep aside covered for about 15 minutes.

Meanwhile, in a small microwave safe bowl, add 3 tbsp. of rice vinegar, sugar and salt and microwave for about 20 seconds.

d. Remove from the microwave and stir till sugar is dissolved.

e. Add vinegar mixture into the bowl of rice and toss to coat well.

f. Keep aside to cool completely.

g. In a bowl, add cucumber, avocado, carrot and crabmeat and toss to coat well.

h. In a small bowl, mix together remaining 2 tbsp. of rice vinegar and soy sauce.

i. In serving bowls, divide the rice evenly.

j. Top with crabmeat mixture and drizzle with soy sauce mixture.

k. Garnish with pickled ginger and sesame seeds and serve.

Truly Asian Sushi Rolls (8 servings, serving: 1 portion)

Per Serving, Calories: 242- Fat: 15g - Carbs: 17.8g - Protein: 12.4g

Ingredients:

- 4¼ cups of water

- 2¼ cups of short-grain brown rice

- 3 tbsp. of mirin

- 3 tbsp. of low-sodium soy sauce

- 3½ tsp. of sugar, divided

- 1/3 cup of rice vinegar

- ½ tsp. of salt

- 8 toasted nori sheets

- 3-ounce of cut into matchstick strips baked tofu

- 1 small cut into matchstick strips red bell pepper

- ½ of peeled, seeded and cut into matchstick strips small cucumber

- 5 tbsp. of chopped unsalted roasted peanuts

Directions:

1. In a large pan, add water on medium heat and bring to a boil.

2. Add rice and stir to combine.

3. Reduce heat to low and simmer, covered for about 50 minutes.

4. Remove from the heat and keep aside, covered for about 10 minutes.

5. Meanwhile in a small skillet, mix together mirin, soy sauce and 1½ tsp. of the sugar and bring to a gentle simmer.

6. Cook for about 3 minutes, stirring continuously.

7. Transfer the warm rice into a large rimmed baking sheet.

8. In a small bowl, add vinegar, remaining 2 tsp. of sugar and salt and beat till well combined.

9. Drizzle the vinegar mixture over the rice and toss to coat well.

10. Place 8 bamboo mats onto a smooth surface.

11. Arrange each nori sheet over a bamboo mat, shiny side down.

12. Place a thin layer of cooled rice over each sheet and press, leaving at least 1-inch top and bottom edge of the sheet uncovered.

13. Drizzle 1 tsp. of the mirin sauce over rice about 1 inch from the bottom,

14. Arrange tofu, bell pepper and cucumber over the sauce and sprinkle with peanuts.

15. Slightly wet the top edge of the seaweed and roll from bottom to the top edge with the help of the bamboo mat tightly.

16. With a sharp knife, cut into desired sized sushi rolls and serve immediately.

Glorious Sushi Rolls (6 servings, serving: 1 portion)

Per Serving, Calories: 358- Fat: 7.6g - Carbs: 55g - Protein: 14.9g

Ingredients:

- 2 cups of rinsed short-grain white rice

- ¼ cup seasoned rice vinegar

- 1 peeled, pitted and mashed avocado

- 1 tbsp. of wasabi

- 1½ tbsp. of finely chopped fresh cilantro

- 24 peeled, cooked and halved crosswise large shrimp

- 6 nori sheets

- 1 tbsp. of minced fresh chives

- 1 peeled, seeded and julienned large carrot

Directions:

1. Prepare the rice according to package's directions.

2. Transfer the rice into a bowl and stir in vinegar.

3. Keep aside in room temperature to cool completely.

4. In a small bowl, mix together mashed avocado and wasabi.

5. In another bowl, mix together cilantro and shrimp.

6. Place 6 bamboo mats onto a smooth surface.

7. Arrange each nori sheet over a bamboo mat, shiny side down.

8. Place a thin layer of cooled rice over each sheet and press, leaving at least 1-inch top and bottom edge of the sheet uncovered.

9. Spread 1 tbsp. of avocado mixture over rice.

10. Arrange 8 shrimp pieces, chives and cucumber strips along bottom third of rice-covered nori.

11. Slightly wet the top edge of the seaweed and roll from bottom to the top edge with the help of the bamboo mat tightly.

12. With a sharp knife, cut into desired sized sushi rolls and serve immediately.

Smoky Flavored Sushi Rolls (4 servings, serving: 1 portion)

Per Serving, Calories: 829- Fat: 50.9g - Carbs: 48.2g - Protein: 41.7g

Ingredients:

- 2 cups of water

- 1 cup of rinsed short grain rice

- 1 tbsp. of rice wine vinegar

- 1 tbsp. of sugar

- 2 Johnsonville smoked bratwurst

- 12 bacon slices

Directions:

1. Prepare grill for two-zone cooking, placing preheated charcoal briquettes on one half of the grill's charcoal grate to create a hot and a cool one.

2. Place the main cooking grate on the grill and adjust the bottom vents to bring the temperature to approximately 350 degrees F.

3. In a pan, add water and rice and place the pan it on the hot side of the grill.

4. Bring the rice to a boil and immediately, cover the pan.

5. Now, place the pan on the cool side of the grill and cook for about 15 minutes.

6. Add the rice wine vinegar and sugar and gently stir to combine.

7. Place the smoked bratwurst on the hot side of the grill and cook for about 3-4 minutes, flipping occasionally.

8. Remove from the grill and keep aside.

9. Arrange a sushi mat onto a smooth surface.

10. Make a bacon weave onto sushi mat, so there are 6 strips lengthwise and 6 strips widthwise.

11. Secure each end with toothpicks to keep bacon from pulling apart.

12. Spread the cooked rice in a ¼-inch thick layer over the bacon weave, leaving about ¼--inch border.

13. Place the bratwurst side by side along the bottom side of the rice.

14. Wrap the sushi tightly and secure with toothpicks.

15. Place the sushi roll onto the cool side of the grill and cover the grill.

16. Cook for about 30 minutes.

17. With a sharp knife, cut into desired sized sushi rolls and serve immediately.

FESTIVE SUSHI ROLLS (4 SERVINGS, SERVING: 1 PORTION)

Per Serving, Calories: 431- Fat: 10.6g - Carbs: 55.7g - Protein: 24.2g

Ingredients:

- 1 cup of water

- 1 cup of rinsed sushi rice

- ¼ cup of mirin seasoning

- 4 cut into strips lengthwise chicken tenderloins

- ¼ cup of sweet chili sauce

- 2 tsp. of olive oil

- 2 tbsp. of mayonnaise

- 4 nori sheets

- ½ of peeled, pitted and thinly sliced medium avocado

- ½ of cut into thin strips Lebanese cucumber

- 1 cup of torn lettuce leaves

Directions:

1. In a pan, add water and rice on medium heat and bring to a boil.

2. Reduce the heat to low and simmer, covered for about 12 minutes.

3. Remove from heat and keep aside, covered for about 10 minutes.

4. Transfer the rice into a large bowl and with a fork, fluff the rice.

5. Slowly, add the seasoning and mix till well combined.

6. Keep aside in the room temperature to cool completely.

7. In a small bowl, add the chicken strips and 2 tbsp. of sweet chili sauce and toss to coat well.

8. In a small frying pan, heat the over medium-high heat.

9. Add chicken and sear the chicken strips for about 5 minutes or till done completely.

10. Meanwhile in a small bowl, mix together mayonnaise and remaining sweet chili sauce.

11. Arrange 4 bamboo mats onto a smooth surface.

12. Arrange 1 nori sheet over each bamboo mat, shiny-side down.

13. Place a thin layer of rice over each sheet and press, leaving at least 1½-inch top and bottom edge of the sheet uncovered.

14. Spread mayonnaise mixture across center of rice.

15. Place chicken, avocado, cucumber and lettuce over rice.

16. Slightly wet the top edge of the sheet and roll from bottom to the top edge with the help of the bamboo mat tightly.

17. With a sharp knife, cut into desired sized sushi rolls and serve immediately.

CREAMY SUSHI ROLLS (4 SERVINGS, SERVING: 1 PORTION)

Per Serving, Calories: 477- Fat: 15.6g - Carbs: 64.6g - Protein: 17.2g

Ingredients:

- 1 cup of cooked and shredded chicken

- 3½ tbsp. of mayonnaise

- 1 tbsp. of Sriracha

- 4 nori sheets

- 1½ cups of cooked sushi rice

- 1 peeled and thinly sliced Persian cucumber

- 1 peeled, pitted and thinly sliced large avocado

Directions:

a. In a bowl, mix together the shredded chicken, mayonnaise and Sriracha.

b. Arrange 4 bamboo mats onto a smooth surface.

c. Arrange 1 nori sheet over each bamboo mat, shiny-side down.

d. Place a thin layer of rice over each sheet and press, leaving at least 1½-inch top and bottom edge of the sheet uncovered.

e. Spread the chicken mixture across center of rice.

f. Top with cucumber and avocado slices.

g. Slightly wet the top edge of the sheet and roll from bottom to the top edge with the help of the bamboo mat tightly.

h. With a sharp knife, cut into desired sized sushi rolls and serve immediately.

Curried Sushi Rolls (2 servings, serving: 1 portion)

Per Serving, Calories: 826- Fat: 41.4g - Carbs: 81g - Protein: 34.8g

Ingredients:

For Rice:

- 3 cups of water

- 1 cup of short grain rice

- ½ tsp. of salt

- ¼ cup of rice wine vinegar

For Chicken:

- 1 tbsp. of olive oil

- 3 (4-ounce) chopped skinless, boneless chicken breasts

- 1 chopped small onion

- 2 minced garlic cloves

- 1 (14-ounce) can of coconut milk

- ¼ cup of raisins

- 1 tbsp. of curry powder

- Salt and freshly ground black pepper, to taste

- 1 tsp. of pine nuts

- 1 tbsp. of chopped fresh cilantro

For Rolls:

- 3 nori sheets

- ½ cup of seeded

- ½ cup of peeled, pitted and thinly sliced avocado

Directions:

1. In a pan, add the water, rice and salt and bring to a boil.

2. Reduce the heat to low and simmer, covered till all the liquid is absorbed.

3. Remove from the heat and stir in the vinegar.

4. Keep aside to cool completely.

5. Meanwhile in a large skillet, heat oil on medium heat.

6. Add chicken and cook till cooked completely.

7. Transfer the chicken into a bowl and keep aside to cool slightly.

8. Chop the chicken finely.

9. In the same skillet, add onion and garlic and sauté for about 2-3 minutes.

10. Add coconut milk and bring to a gentle boil.

11. Add the cooked chicken, raisins, curry powder, salt, pepper, pine nuts and cilantro and simmer for about 10-15 minutes.

12. Remove from heat and keep aside to cool completely.

13. Arrange 2 bamboo mats onto a smooth surface.

14. Arrange 1 nori sheet over each bamboo mat, shiny-side down.

15. Place a thin layer of rice over each sheet and press, leaving at least 1½-inch top and bottom edge of the sheet uncovered.

16. Place the curried chicken salad horizontally across the roll.

17. Top with bell pepper and avocado.

18. Slightly wet the top edge of the sheet and roll from bottom to the top edge with the help of the bamboo mat tightly.

19. With a sharp knife, cut into desired sized sushi rolls and serve immediately.

AROMATIC SUSHI ROLLS (4 SERVINGS, SERVING: 1 PORTION)

Per Serving, Calories: 554- Fat: 7.9g - Carbs: 89.1g - Protein: 27.5g

Ingredients:

- 14-ounce of trimmed and cut into 8 slices beef fillet

- ¼ cup of teriyaki sauce, divided

- 8 trimmed green shallots

- 1 peeled and sliced into long thin strips medium carrot

- 4 nori sheets

- 2 cup of cooked brown rice

- 2 tsp. of finely grated fresh ginger

- 1 tbsp. of fresh lemon juice

- 1 tbsp. of minced fresh chives

Directions:

1. In a bowl, mix together beef and 2 tbsp. of teriyaki sauce.

2. Keep aside for about 30 minutes.

3. Preheat the grill to high heat. Grease the grill grate.

4. Grill the beef strips for about 2 minutes per side.

5. Remove from the grill and keep aside for about 4-5 minutes.

6. Now, grill the shallots and carrots for about 1-2 minutes.

7. Remove from the grill and keep aside.

8. Arrange 4 bamboo mats onto a smooth surface.

9. Arrange 1 nori sheet over each bamboo mat, shiny-side down.

10. Place a thin layer of rice over each sheet and press, leaving at least 1½-inch top and bottom edge of the sheet uncovered.

11. Place 2 beef slices, 2 shallots and several carrot sticks on lower part of each nori sheet.

12. Slightly wet the top edge of the sheet and roll from bottom to the top edge with the help of the bamboo mat tightly.

13. With a sharp knife, cut into desired sized sushi rolls and serve immediately.

FAMILY DINNER SUSHI ROLLS (2 SERVINGS, SERVING: 1 PORTION)

Per Serving, Calories: 500- Fat: 10.2g - Carbs: 66.8g - Protein: 32.5g

Ingredients:

For Sushi Rolls:

- 4-ounce of rinsed sushi rice

- 2 tbsp. of mirin

- 2 nori sheets

- 6-ounce of cut into long strips cooked beef

- 2 tsp. of mayonnaise

- 2 tsp. of wasabi paste

- 1 peeled and cut into thin strips small carrot

- ½ of peeled and cut into thin strips small cucumber

- ½ of seeded and cut into thin strips small red bell pepper

For Dressing:

- ½ tbsp. of soy sauce

- ¼ tbsp. of rice wine vinegar

- ½ tsp. of sesame oil

- 1 tsp. of melted honey

- ½ tsp. of wasabi paste

- 1 tbsp. of finely chopped pickled ginger

Directions:

1. Prepare the sushi rice according to package's directions.

2. Remove from the heat and keep aside, covered to cool.

3. Meanwhile for dressing in a small bowl, mix together all the ingredients.

4. Arrange 2 bamboo mats onto a smooth surface.

5. Arrange 1 nori sheet over each bamboo mat, shiny-side down.

6. Spread rice over each nori sheet in an even layer, leaving a ½-inch border.

7. Drizzle with the mirin evenly.

8. Arrange the beef, carrot, cucumber and pepper in a strip along the length of the rice.

9. Top with the wasabi in the form of dots.

10. Slightly wet the top edge of the sheet and roll from bottom to the top edge with the help of the bamboo mat tightly.

11. With a sharp knife, cut into desired sized sushi rolls and serve immediately.

WEEKEND DINNER SUSHI ROLLS (6 SERVINGS, SERVING: 1 PORTION)

Per Serving, Calories: 491- Fat: 10.9g - Carbs: 55.8g - Protein: 38g

Ingredients:

- 2 cups plus 3 tbsp. of water, divided

- 2 cups of rinsed white rice

- 2 tbsp. of cider vinegar

- 2 chard leaves

- 2 tbsp. of cider vinegar

- 2 chard leaves

- 2 beaten eggs

- 2 tbsp. of soy sauce, divided

- 1 tbsp. of vegetable oil

- 1 chopped onion

- ¾ pound of lean ground beef

- 1 (5-ounce) can of drained tuna

- 1 peeled and julienned cucumber

- 1 peeled and julienned carrot

- 6 nori sheets

Directions:

1. In a medium pan, add 2 cups of water and cider vinegar and bring to a boil.

2. Add rice and stir to combine.

3. Reduce heat and simmer, covered for about 20 minutes.

4.   Meanwhile in another medium pan of water, cook the chard till tender.

5.   Drain well and cut into thin strips.

6.   In a bowl, add the eggs, 1 tbsp. of soy sauce and 3 tbsp. of water and beat till well combined.

7.   Heat a medium frying pan on medium heat.

8.   Add the egg mixture and cook till set completely.

9.   Remove from heat and cut into strips.

10. In a skillet, heat the vegetable oil on medium-high heat.

11. Add the onion and sauté till tender.

12. Stir in the beef and 1 tbsp. of soy sauce and cook till browned completely.

13. Remove from the heat and drain the excess grease.

14. Arrange 6 bamboo mats onto a smooth surface.

15. Arrange 1 nori sheet over each bamboo mat, shiny-side down.

16. Place a thin layer of rice over each sheet and press, leaving at least 1½-inch top and bottom edge of the sheet uncovered.

17. Top the rice with a strip of egg, a stick of carrot, a line of tuna, a cucumber slice and a line of beef.

18. Repeat till the food reaches in the middle of the nori sheet.

19. Slightly wet the top edge of the sheet and roll from bottom to the top edge with the help of the bamboo mat tightly.

20. With a sharp knife, cut into desired sized sushi rolls and serve immediately.

FAMILY FAVORITE SUSHI ROLLS (4 SERVINGS, SERVING: 1 PORTION)

Per Serving, Calories: 483- Fat: 14.9g - Carbs: 44.1g - Protein: 16.2g

Ingredients:

- 1½ cups of water, divided

- 1 cup of rinsed white rice

- 1 tbsp. of sesame oil

- Salt, to taste

- 1 tsp. of olive oil

- 2 beaten eggs

- 4 nori sheets

- 1 peeled and cut into thin strips carrot

- 1 peeled and cut into thin strips cucumber

- 4 cut into thin strips American cheese slices

- 4 cut into thin strips cooked ham slices

Directions:

1. In a pan, add water and rice and bring to a boil.

2. Reduce the heat to low and simmer, covered till all the liquid is absorbed.

3. Transfer the cooked rice onto a baking sheet and keep aside to cool.

4. Stir in 1 tbsp. of sesame oil and salt.

5. Meanwhile in a frying pan, heat oil on medium-high heat.

6. Add eggs and cook till set completely, without stirring.

7. Remove from heat and cut into strips.

8. Arrange 4 bamboo mats onto a smooth surface.

9. Arrange 1 nori sheet over each bamboo mat, shiny-side down.

10. Place a thin layer of rice over each sheet and press, leaving at least 1½-inch top and bottom edge of the sheet uncovered.

11. Slightly wet the top edge of the sheet and roll from bottom to the top edge with the help of the bamboo mat tightly.

12. With a sharp knife, cut into desired sized sushi rolls and serve immediately.

SEAFOOD LOVER'S SUSHI ROLLS (2 SERVINGS, SERVING: 1 PORTION)

Per Serving, Calories: 861- Fat: 35.1g - Carbs: 105.9g - Protein: 27.4g

Ingredients:

- 2/3 cup of mayonnaise

- 2 tbsp. of Sriracha chili sauce

- 2-ounce of chopped salmon

- 2-ounce of peeled, deveined and chopped shrimp

- 2-ounce of chopped scallops

- 1 cups of cooked sushi rice

- 2 tbsp. of rice vinegar

- 1 tsp. of powdered sugar

- Pinch of salt

- 2 nori sheets

- ¼ of peeled and sliced into thin strips English cucumber

- 6 scallions, divided

- 2 tbsp. of softened cream cheese

- 1 tbsp. of toasted sesame seeds

Directions:

1. Pre-heat the oven to 350 degrees F. Line a baking sheet with a large piece of foil.

2. In a bowl, add mayonnaise and Srirachaa and beat till well combined.

3. Add seafood and toss to coat well.

4. Spread the seafood onto the prepared baking sheet.

5. Roll up the edges of foil a bit over the seafood

6. Bake for about 15 minutes.

7. In a bowl, add rice vinegar, sugar and salt and stir to combine well.

8. Arrange 2 bamboo mats onto a smooth surface.

9. Arrange 1 nori sheet over each bamboo mat, shiny-side down.

10. Place a thin layer of rice over each sheet and press, leaving at least 1½-inch top and bottom edge of the sheet uncovered.

11. Place cucumber, scallion and cream cheese in three compact rows at the end of the seaweed square over the rice.

12. Slightly wet the top edge of the sheet and roll from bottom to the top edge with the help of the bamboo mat tightly.

13. Sprinkle with the sesame seeds.

14. With a sharp knife, cut into desired sized sushi rolls and serve immediately.

LIVELY FLAVORED SUSHI ROLLS (6 SERVINGS, SERVING: 1 PORTION)

Per Serving, Calories: 842- Fat: 15.4g - Carbs: 142.4g - Protein: 29.8g

Ingredients:

- ¼ cup of mayonnaise

- 4 tsp. of brown sugar

- 4 tsp. of fresh lemon juice

- 1 pound of drained and patted dry with paper towels lump crabmeat

- 5 cups of cooked sushi rice

- ¼ cup of seasoned rice vinegar

- 6 nori sheets

- 1 peeled, pitted and cut into thin slices large mango

- 1 peeled, pitted and cut into thin slices large avocado

- 1 seeded and cut into thin slices small red bell pepper

- ¼ cup of black sesame seeds

Directions:

1. In a medium bowl, mix together the mayonnaise, sugar and lemon juice.

2. Add crabmeat and mix till well combined.

3. In another bowl, mix together rice and vinegar.

4. Arrange 5 bamboo mats onto a smooth surface.

5. Arrange 1 nori sheet over each bamboo mat, shiny-side down.

6. Place a thin layer of rice over each sheet and press, leaving at least 1½-inch top and bottom edge of the sheet uncovered.

7. Arrange the crab mixture along the center of the nori leaving a 2-inch border over the rice.

8. Top the crab mixture with avocado, mango slices and bell pepper slices.

9. Slightly wet the top edge of the sheet and roll from bottom to the top edge with the help of the bamboo mat tightly.

10. Sprinkle with the sesame seeds.

11. With a sharp knife, cut into desired sized sushi rolls and serve immediately.

MEXICAN INSPIRED SUSHI ROLLS (3 SERVINGS, SERVING: 1 PORTION)

Per Serving, Calories: 532- Fat: 30.9g - Carbs: 52.7g - Protein: 16.5g

Ingredients:

- 3-ounce of softened cream cheese

- 1 ½ tbsp. of seeded and finely chopped chipotle in adobo

- 3 warmed large flour tortillas

- ¾ cup of refried lack beans

- 1/3 cup of salsa

- 1½ of peeled, pitted and chopped avocados

- ¾ cup of chopped fresh cilantro

Directions:

1. In a bowl, mix together cream cheese and chipotle.

2. Spread cream cheese over each tortilla evenly.

3. Top with black beans, salsa, avocado and cilantro evenly.

4. Roll up each tortillas tightly.

5. With a sharp knife, cut into desired sized sushi rolls and serve immediately.

Chapter 4: Snack & Dessert Recipes

Crunchy Sushi Rolls (2 servings, serving: 1 portion)

Per Serving, Calories: 380- Fat: 26g - Carbs: 35.2g - Protein: 8.8g

Ingredients:

For Rolls:

- ½ of thinly sliced medium zucchini

- Salt, to taste

- ½ of peeled and julienned carrot

- 1/3 of peeled, seeded and julienned cucumber

- ½ of seeded and julienned green bell pepper

- ½ of cored and julienned apple

- 1 thinly sliced scallion

For Pesto:

- 1 peeled, pitted and chopped avocado

- 1/3 cup of roughly chopped cashews

- 1/3 cup of roughly chopped almonds

- 1 chopped garlic clove

- 1 tbsp. of olive oil

- 1 tbsp. of fresh lemon juice

- 1 tsp. of balsamic vinegar

- Pinch of salt

Directions:

1. In a colander, add the zucchini and sprinkle with salt.

2. Arrange the colander in a sink till zucchini becomes soft.

3. Meanwhile for pesto in a blender, add all ingredients and pulse till smooth.

4. Rinse the zucchini well to remove the extra salt.

5. With paper towels, pat dry the zucchini.

6. Spread the pesto over each zucchini slices at both ends.

7. Place the veggies on top and carefully, roll tightly around the filling.

8. Secure with the toothpicks and serve immediately.

DISTINCTIVE SUSHI ROLLS (12 SERVINGS, SERVING: 1 PORTION)

Per Serving, Calories: 48- Fat: 3.3g - Carbs: 4.1g - Protein: 1g

Ingredients:

- 1 trimmed seedless cucumber

- 1 peeled and shredded carrot

- 1 (4-ounce) package of softened cream cheese

- ¼ cup of raisins

Directions:

1. With a peeler, slice cucumber into 8 1/8-inch thick slices lengthwise.

2. Cut each slice into 3 pieces crosswise.

3. Arrange 1 tsp. of shredded carrot onto the bottom edge of each cucumber slice.

4. Place 1 tsp. of cream cheese over the carrot and press 2-3 raisins into the cream cheese.

5. Roll the cucumber slice into a little sushi roll, starting at the filled end.

6. Secure with toothpicks and serve.

UNIQUE SUSHI SNACK (4 SERVINGS, SERVING: 1 PORTION)

Per Serving, Calories: 533- Fat: 20.6g - Carbs: 78.2g - Protein: 11.1g

Ingredients:

- 2 cups of rinsed brown rice

- 2 tbsp. of olive oil

- 2 tbsp. of tahini

- 2 finely sliced scallions

- 1 tsp. of finely grated fresh ginger

- 1/3 cup of sesame seeds, divided

- 1 tbsp. of poppy seeds

Directions:

1. In a rice cooker, cook the rice following the instructions and adding the extra ¼ cup of the water.

2. Transfer the cooked rice into a bowl and keep aside slightly.

3. In warm rice, add tahini, olive oil, scallion, ginger, ¼ cup of sesame seeds and poppy seeds and mix well.

4. In a shallow dish, place the remaining sesame seeds.

5. With wet hands first, make small balls from the mixture.

6. Coat each ball with sesame seeds evenly and serve.

VERSATILE SUSHI SNACK (4 SERVINGS, SERVING: 1 PORTION)

Per Serving, Calories: 455- Fat: 11.5g - Carbs: 76.1g - Protein: 12.6g

Ingredients:

- 3 cups of water

- 2 cups of rinsed brown sushi rice

- ½ tsp. of fine salt

- ¼ cup of sesame seeds

- 3 tbsp. of toasted and chopped almonds

- ¼ cup of minced scallion

- 2 scrambled and cut into shreds eggs

Directions:

1. In a pan, add water and rice on medium-high heat and bring to a boil.

2. Reduce the heat to medium-low and simmer, covered for about 1 hour.

3. Remove the rice from heat and keep aside, covered for at least 15 minutes.

4. With a fork, fluff the rice.

5. Slowly, add the sesame seeds, almonds and scallions and stir to combine.

6. Line a small cup with plastic wrap and drizzle with a dash of water.

7. Fill the cup 2/3 full with rice mixture.

8. With a finger, insert a little egg in the center of the ball.

9. Carefully remove plastic wrap and set the rice ball in a parchment lined plate.

10. Repeat with the remaining rice and eggs.

KID'S FRIENDLY SUSHI ROLLS (2 SERVING, SERVING: 1 PORTION)

Per Serving, Calories: 262- Fat: 9.2g - Carbs: 44.3g - Protein: 9.3g

Ingredients:

- 1 peeled banana

- 1½ tbsp. of plain Greek yogurt

- 2 tbsp. of sprinkles

- 2 tbsp. of fresh blackberries

Directions:

1. With a butter knife, spread a layer of Greek yogurt over the outside surface of the banana.

2. In a shallow dish, place the sprinkles.

3. Coat the banana with sprinkles evenly.

4. Cut into sushi sized pieces.

5. In a serving plate, arrange the banana slices.

6. Top with blackberries and serve.

CHOCOLATE LOVER'S SUSHI TREAT (4 SERVINGS, SERVING: 1 PORTION)

Per Serving, Calories: 245- Fat: 13.4g - Carbs: 30g - Protein: 19.1g

Ingredients:

- 2 peeled bananas

- ½ cup of melted dark chocolate

- 1 cup of chopped pistachio

Directions:

1. Stick a toothpick at both ends of each banana.

2. Cover with the bananas with melted chocolate then sprinkle with the chopped pistachios.

3. Freeze for a couple of minutes or till the chocolate becomes set.

4. Cut the bananas into bite-sized sushi pieces and serve.

YUMMY SUSHI ROLLS (2 SERVINGS, SERVING: 1 PORTION)

Per Serving, Calories: 268- Fat: 18.1g - Carbs: 22.6g - Protein: 9g

Ingredients:

- 1 peeled large banana

- ¼ cup of peanut butter

- 2 tbsp. of shredded coconut

Directions:

1. Cut the banana into bite-sized sushi pieces

2. With an apple corer, remove the middle part of the banana slices.

3. Fill each hollowed banana with peanut butter.

4. Sprinkle with the coconut and serve.

ENTERTAINING SUSHI ROLLS (8 SERVINGS, SERVING: 1 PORTION)

Per Serving, Calories: 186- Fat: 13.1g - Carbs: 16.5g - Protein: 2.7g

Ingredients:

- 1½ cups of coconut milk

- ½ cup of rinsed white rice

- 2 tbsp. of white sugar

- ½ cup of hulled and sliced fresh strawberries

- ¼ cup of black sesame seeds

Directions:

1. In a small pan, add coconut milk, rice and sugar on high heat and bring to a boil.

2. Reduce the heat to low and simmer, covered for about 18-20 minutes.

3. Remove from the heat and with a fork, fluff the rice.

4. Keep aside to cool completely.

5. Cover a bamboo mat with a plastic wrap.

6. Place the rice in the middle of the bamboo mat and top with the strawberries at the center.

7. Roll the sushi with the help of the sushi mat and with the plastic wrap, tighten into a cylinder.

8. Unwrap the plastic wrap and with a sharp knife, slice the rice to bite sized sushi rolls.

9. Coat the sushi pieces with the sesame seeds and serve.

Fruit Lover's Sushi Rolls (12 servings, serving: 1 portion)

Per Serving, Calories: 83- Fat: 2.6g - Carbs: 17.5g - Protein: 1g

Ingredients:

For Rolls:

- 1 cored and cut into matchsticks apple

- 1 tsp. of fresh lemon juice

- 6 rice paper wrappers

- 2 peeled and cut into thin slices kiwis

- 8 hulled and cut into thin slices fresh strawberries

- 1 peeled, pitted and cut into matchsticks mango

- 1 cup fresh baby spinach

For Chocolate Sauce:

- ¼ cup of heavy cream

- ¼ cup of semisweet chocolate chips

Directions:

1. In a small bowl, add apple and lemon juice and toss to coat well.

2. Keep aside till using.

3. In a large bowl, add warm water and soak the rice paper wraps for about 20-30 seconds or till pliable, but still slightly firm.

4. Arrange the rice paper wraps onto a cutting board, smooth side down.

5. Arrange the fruits on one half of each wrap.

6. Fold the wrappers over the filling and carefully roll like a cylinder.

7. For sauce in a microwave safe bowl, add the heavy cream and microwave for about 30-40 seconds.

8. Place the cream over the chocolate chips and keep aside for about 1 minute.

9. Stir till mixture becomes smooth.

10. With a sharp knife, cut into desired sized sushi rolls.

11. Coat each roll with the chocolate sauce and serve.

ULTIMATE SUMMER SUSHI TREAT (12 SERVINGS, SERVING: 1 PORTION)

Per Serving, Calories: 104- Fat: 1.4g - Carbs: 22.2g - Protein: 1.6g

Ingredients:

- 1 cup of rinsed and soaked for 30 minutes sushi rice

- 1¼ cups of water

- ¼ cup of coconut milk

- ¼ cup of sugar

- ¼ tsp. of salt

- 1 tbsp. of honey

- 12 thin slices of kiwi

- 1 cup seeded and chopped orange

- 6 halved fresh raspberries

Directions:

1. In a medium pan, add rice and water and bring to a boil.

2. Reduce the heat and simmer, covered for about 15 minutes.

3. Remove from heat and keep aside, covered for about 15 minutes.

4. Transfer the rice in a large bowl.

5. Add sugar, coconut milk and salt and gently, stir to combine.

6. Keep aside, covered for about 20 minutes.

7. With lightly, greased hands, make 12 equal sized balls from the mixture.

8. Lightly press each rice ball into an oval between palms.

9. Arrange the ovals onto a wax paper lined baking sheet.

10. Coat the balls with honey slightly.

11. Top each rice oval with kiwi slice, orange and raspberry slice.

12. Cover and refrigerate to chill for about 8 hours before serving.

School Snack Sushi Rolls (4 servings, serving: 1 portion)

Per Serving, Calories: 92- Fat: 0.7g - Carbs: 25.7g - Protein: 1g

Ingredients:

- 2 large flour tortillas

- ¼ cup of peanut butter

- ¼ cup of strawberry jam

- 2 peeled bananas

Directions:

1. Spread peanut butter followed by jam over each tortilla evenly.

2. Arrange 1 peeled banana along the side of each tortilla and roll up jellyroll style.

3. Cover tightly with plastic wrap, twisting the ends.

4. Cut into desired sushi rolls and serve.

SUSHI ROLLS (2 SERVINGS, SERVING: 1 PORTION)

Per Serving, Calories: 346- Fat: 20g - Carbs: 34.7g - Protein: 8.1g

Ingredients:

- 1 rice paper wrapper

- 3 tbsp. of almond butter

- ¼ cup of shredded sweetened coconut

- 3 tbsp. of mini chocolate chips

- 2 very thinly sliced strawberries

- 1 halved lengthwise large banana

- 2 tbsp. of strawberry yogurt

Directions:

1. Arrange the wrapper onto a smooth surface.

2. Spread the almond butter across half of the wrap all the way to the edge.

3. Sprinkle the coconut and chocolate covered chips evenly across the top of the peanut butter.

4. Arrange strawberries next to each other on top of the coconut in a straight line, leaving about 1-inch of an overhang from the top of the wrap.

5. Repeat this process creating a second line of strawberries.

6. Arrange the banana on top of the strawberries.

7. Carefully, roll the wrap and gently, seal it.

8. With a sharp knife, cut into desired sized sushi rolls.

9. Drizzle with yogurt and serve.

SWEET-TOOTH CARVING SUSHI TREAT (10 SERVINGS, SERVING: 1 PORTION)

Per Serving, Calories: 197- Fat: 2.8g - Carbs: 39.5g - Protein: 3.4g

Ingredients:

- 1 tbsp. of unsalted butter

- 2/3 cup of mini marshmallows

- 2 cups of cooked white rice

- 1 peeled and thinly sliced banana

- 2 cups of hulled and sliced fresh strawberries

- ¼ cup of mini chocolate chips

Directions:

1. In a medium pan, melt the butter and marshmallows on medium-low heat till completely soft.

2. Remove from the heat and stir in the cooked rice till well combined.

3. In a bowl, mix together banana and strawberry slices.

4. Lightly, grease an ice cube tray.

5. In the bottom of ice cube tray, divide the fruit mixture.

6. Top with the rice and press gently into the fruit.

7. Unmold the sushi and top with the chocolate chips and serve.

PARTY-TIME SUSHI TREAT (12 SERVINGS, SERVING: 1 PORTION)

Per Serving, Calories: 208- Fat: 5.6g - Carbs: 11.8g - Protein: 3.1g

Ingredients:

- 1 cup of pancake mix

- ¾ cup of milk

- ¼ cup of water

- 1 large egg

- 1 tbsp. of canola oil

- 12 tbsp. of softened strawberry cream cheese

- 2 cups of hulled and quartered fresh strawberries

- ¼ cup of crushed cocoa puffs cereal

Directions:

1. In a bowl, add the pancake mix, milk, water, egg and oil and mix till well combined.

2. Heat a lightly greased 8-inch nonstick skillet on low heat.

3. Place about ½ cup of the mixture into the skillet and tilt the pan to spread evenly in the bottom of the skillet.

4. Cook for about 2 minutes per side.

5. Transfer the pancake onto a plate to cool.

6. Repeat with the remaining mixture.

7. Arrange 4 bamboo mats onto a smooth surface.

8. Place 1 pancake over each bamboo mat.

9. Spread 3 tbsp. of cream cheese over each pancake, leaving the top 2-inches bare.

10. Place ½ cup of strawberry slices in a line across the middle.

11. Slightly wet the top edge of the sheet and roll from bottom to the top edge with the help of the bamboo mat tightly.

12. With a sharp knife, cut into desired sized sushi rolls.

13. Sprinkle with puff cereal and serve immediately.

SATISFYING SUSHI TREAT (12 SERVINGS, SERVING: 1 PORTION)

Per Serving, Calories: 233- Fat: 6.5g - Carbs: 37.6g - Protein: 6.8g

Ingredients:

- 6 cups of water

- ½ tsp. of salt

- 2 cups of steel-cut oats

- 1 cup of pancake mix

- ¾ cup of milk

- ¼ cup of water

- 1 large egg

- 1 tbsp. of canola oil

- 12 tbsp. of Nutella

- 4 peeled bananas

- 1 cup of coconut flakes

Directions:

1. In a pan, add water and salt and bring to a boil.

2. Add oats and stir to combine.

3. Reduce the heat and cook for about 10-20 minutes, stirring occasionally.

4. Meanwhile for the pancakes in a bowl, add the pancake mix, milk, water, egg and oil and mix till well combined.

5. Heat a lightly greased 8-inch nonstick skillet on low heat.

6. Place about ½ cup of the mixture into the skillet and tilt the pan to spread evenly in the bottom of the skillet.

7. Cook for about 2 minutes per side.

8. Transfer the pancake onto a plate to cool.

9. Repeat with the remaining mixture.

10. Arrange 4 bamboo mats onto a smooth surface

11. Spread ¼ of the oatmeal in an even layer over each the bamboo mat.

12. Place a pancake on top.

13. Spread 3 tbsp. of Nutella in the middle section of the pancake, leaving the top and bottom 2-inches bare.

14. Place1 banana across the middle and sprinkle with coconut flakes line next to it.

15. Pull the bottom of the mat up to help roll the oatmeal and pancake over the filling.

16. With a sharp knife, cut into desired sized sushi rolls.

17. Sprinkle with coconut and serve immediately.

CONCLUSION

Thank you again for picking up this cookbook! I hope it was able to help you to find a wide variety of healthy, and delicious sounding recipes that you can't wait to try for yourself.

Finally, if you enjoyed this book, then I'd like to ask you for a favor, would you be kind enough to leave a review for this book on Amazon? It'd be greatly appreciated!

Printed in Great Britain
by Amazon